GOD
on the
Black Market

Michael Lowery

TATE PUBLISHING, LLC

"God on the Black Market" by Michael Lowery
Copyright © 2005 by Michael Lowery. All rights reserved.

Published in the United States of America
by Tate Publishing, LLC
127 East Trade Center Terrace
Mustang, OK 73064
(888) 361–9473

Book design copyright © 2005 by Tate Publishing, LLC. All rights reserved.

No part of this publication may be reproduced, stored in a retrieval system or transmitted in any way by any means, electronic, mechanical, photocopy, recording or otherwise without the prior permission of the author except as provided by USA copyright law.

Scripture quotations marked "KJV" are taken from the *Holy Bible, King James Version,* Cambridge, 1769.

This book is designed to provide accurate and authoritative information with regard to the subject matter covered. This information is given with the understanding that neither the author nor Tate Publishing, LLC is engaged in rendering legal, professional advice. Since the details of your situation are fact dependent, you should additionally seek the services of a competent professional.

ISBN: 1–5988602–5-9

Dedication

This book is dedicated to two very important people who saw the "author" in me long before I ever did. Their encouraging words inspired me to follow my dreams of becoming a writer and never to give up. Their influence reminds all of us never to underestimate the impact a schoolteacher can have on a child, especially at an early age. To Mr. John Derry, a teacher in the Gifted and Talented Program at Jackie Robinson Middle School in New Haven, CT, and Mrs. Conte, my fourth grade teacher at Timothy Dwight Elementary School, New Haven, CT. It was Mr. Derry who assisted me in writing my very first book called "Trouble with John Lumely." This sparked a flame that was fanned by the encouraging words of Mrs. Conte. Although they have been far removed from my life for nearly three decades, their impact has been permanent. I owe them dearly. To the both of you, I say, "Thank you!"

Acknowledgments

Sincere appreciation goes out to Stephanie, my beloved wife of over 14 years, especially for your unwavering support and commitment to praying for me as I poured my heart and soul into this book. Thank you for allowing me the time and focus required to complete such an overwhelming task. I thank God for your patience and diligence in maintaining a wonderful home for our two beautiful children, Myles and Layke-Michal, especially during the countless hours of pastoral ministry, music ministry, and now authorship.

Thank you also to my administrative assistant, Jenean George, for your untiring efforts in insuring this book's successful completion.

I also want to acknowledge Carol Daniels who served as my personal preliminary editor to make sure my thoughts would make sense to people other than me. Thank you, Carol, for your spirit of excellence!

I also want to acknowledge the contributions of Pastor Sean Teal! Thank you for sharing your thoughts of this book with the world. You are truly a gift to the Body of Christ!

Thank you to the staff at Tate Publishing for

your belief in the message of the book, especially for your belief in me.

Finally, thank you to the Berean Christian Fellowship Church family for your continued support. Serving you as pastor is truly an honor!

Table of Contents

Foreword................................ 9

Introduction–*God on the Black Market* 13

Chapter One–*Bootlegging the Bible* 15
The Bootleg Breach 22
The Bondage of Bootlegging 27
"What is Truth?"........................ 30

Chapter Two–*Christianity in Crisis* 37
Materialism and Commercialism 40
Consumerism 45
The "How-to" Church.................... 49

Chapter Three–*"A House of Prayer" or a
"Den of Thieves"* 53
If My People............................ 57
The Livestock Market.................... 63
Turning the Tables....................... 67

Chapter Four–*The Temple of God*............ 73
Holy Ground 78
A House of Prayer....................... 81
A House of Power....................... 87
A House of Perfected Praise 91

Chapter Five–*Identity Theft* 97
The Temptation in the Wilderness 101
Fraud................................. 107

Power Starvation 111

Chapter Six–*Identity Crisis* 119
"Who Are We to Judge?" 123
Saint or Sinner Saved by Grace? 128
Bribery 132

Chapter Seven–*Closing the Gates!* 137
Marketing and Merchandising Misery 143
Panhandling and Peddling Pain 146
The Spiritual Hustle 149
The Children's Bread 152
The Wounded Healer 155

Chapter Eight–*The Counterfeit Conspiracy* 159
Of God or Men 164
Covenant or Covet-Knit 168
Exposing an Imposter 171
Profit Gains and Losses 174
The Delilah Device 178

Chapter Nine–*The Spreading Democracy* 185
Spiritual Suffrage 189
The Popular Vote 191
The Electoral Vote 193
"Bye"-Partisanship 195

Foreword

Jesus invested the revelation of the Kingdom in parabolic terms, which paralleled with economic realities. Matthew records the Master teaching, "The kingdom of God is like unto a merchant man, seeking goodly pearls: who, when he had found one pearl of great price, went and sold all that he had, and bought it" (Matthew 13:45–46). The Kingdom of God is the eternal economy of God, which has come into the world to interrupt and intercept man's fleeting political systems and failing economic strategies. Jesus clearly and squarely places the Kingdom as the most valuable commodity in the human experience. Anything that we have in the portfolios of our pursuits and purposes that is less than the Kingdom should be bartered away in order to obtain the better and the best that God offers. The exchange to be made is costly and will redefine the future of the investor. The Kingdom of God is an expensive enterprise. It will cost you everything. There are no sales, bargains, or rebates in God's economy. The Kingdom will correct any man or market that attempts to get God and the gospel on the black market.

Pastor Michael Lowery has written a book that exposes the subtle fluctuations in the modern-day gospel presentations that offer Christianity in the cheapest packaging possible. This book, however, is much more than a critique of the contemporary church. This book is a clarion call to the church and its clergy to return to the costly gospel that left Heaven bankrupt while the Prince of Life purchased our redemption upon the cruel cross of Calvary. It is the costly gospel that will inspire this generation to live for something more than the next boatload of blessings and the plethora of prosperity principles that are presented as panaceas for the anxiety of our age.

This book will be of special interest to those who want to develop a deep and abiding connection to the church. Pastor Lowery helps the new and young believer by offering foundations that are spiritual and sure, not traditional or trendy. He helps the more seasoned saint see the sickness of a system that most experienced church people have been lulled to accept as the outgrowth of religious evolution. Those who again want to trust the church and its leaders will find a comforting voice and a challenging word in the writings of Pastor Lowery.

As you move from page to page, you will find that Pastor Lowery has stained this book with the blood of his prophetic burden and pastoral care. He writes as one who lives in the church, looks at the church, and loves the church. Those who want more from the church and its leaders than motivational speakers and user-friendly services will find this book to be a necessary correction and compass for the 21st Century Church. Pastor Lowery does not seek to resolve all the issues raised by the truths he presents. He leaves the reader with a necessary tension. He makes his case with a compelling merger of biblical expositions and personal illustrations. The jury of your soul will now have to bring back a verdict. Are God, the gospel, and the Kingdom worth the purchase price as marked in the Scriptures?

Bishop Sean Teal

Introduction

There is a dangerous component that I have discovered to be an epidemic in the Body of Christ. It seems that when listening closely to sermons and reading literature circulating in many secular and religious circles, God is being marketed in a way that makes Him acceptable to the modern-day "Christian" and palatable to a twenty-first-century Western culture that sees the Bible as archaic and simply passé. I was surprised at the misguided theological beliefs of many churchgoers and how every culture seeks to make God relative to its lifestyle. It is possible to have thousands of congregants attending one service, with most of them not agreeing on who God really is. Although this confusion can be cleared up in a matter of moments from the pulpit, it isn't. Rather, it is brushed over with a stroke of ingenious marketing savvy, as sermons are replaced with noncommittal speeches that are designed to "motivate" and "inspire," rather than convict unto righteousness.

What have we sacrificed for the sake of quantitative growth? What concepts have we compromised for the sake of acceptance into the mainstream? What have we embraced in order to be "progressive" and "relevant"? What foundational truths have we forsaken for the sake of political correctness? What doctrinal truths have we diluted for the purposes of "tolerance"? It appears as though we have placed God in an irreverent, immoral system-of-trade in order to make Him "affordable" and "appealing" to any and all standards.

As a result, the perception of God has become severely diluted because we have "black-marketed" Him, funneling Him through the ideologies of everyone and anyone who dares to say they are a "Christian." This book examines the reasons and results of trying to receive "God on the Black Market."

Chapter I

BOOTLEGGING THE BIBLE

It is ironic that although we are living in a time of uncontrolled sexual immorality, uninhibited exhibitionism, and uncensored images across the airways, the Bible, along with other Christian literature, continues to be among our nation's top sellers each and every year. It is because having the Bible in circulation has never influenced a culture. The Bible *in application* influences a culture! We must conclude that the only way there can be worldwide application of the Holy Scriptures, is if the interpretation and translation are universal. Meaning, if the Bible's translations and interpretations are lost in an abyss of relativism, then the world can never experience worldwide application because everyone would see the Word differently.

The enemy to appropriating the promises in the Bible is avoiding the principles of the Bible. That is easily done when the scriptures are misinterpreted and misappropriated for the sake of compromise and convenience. It is easy to attract any kind of lifestyle when the Bible is unofficially revised. The unofficial, unauthorized revision of scripture in order to accommodate any and all lifestyles is what I coin "Bootlegging the Bible." It is a second and third generation reproduction of the original version in order to avoid the cost of adhering to its original standard.

Bootlegging the Bible requires someone consciously to compromise the integrity of scriptural clarity in order to gain a profit. It is a result of a spirit or mindset that wants something for nothing. It is the effort of an individual who seeks to receive the promises of God's provisions while revising the premise of God's principles. Any spirit that embraces the theory of the Bible as not being absolute truth, as there being a margin for error, as God not being the God of the Bible but rather a more modern, tolerant God, is a rebellious spirit that seeks to bootleg the Holy Scriptures.

The Bible declares in 2 Timothy 3:16 "All scripture is given by inspiration of God, and is profitable for doctrine, for reproof, for correction, for instruction in righteousness: That the man of God may be perfect, thoroughly furnished unto all good works." The word inspired (Gk.theopneustos) comes from two Greek words: theos, meaning "God," and pneo, meaning "to breathe." Thus "inspired" means "God-breathed." All scripture is therefore God-breathed; it is the very life and Word of God. The Bible is without error, absolutely true, trustworthy, and infallible.[1] Notice what Paul tells Timothy here in 2 Timothy 3:16. Every benefit he mentions here falls under the category of discipline. He declares that scripture is profitable for doctrine, reproof, correction, for instruction in righteousness. It is no coincidence that you do not find any pleasurable superlatives mentioned here. Each word represents a level of discipline.

First of all, doctrine is the foundational cornerstone to all beliefs. It serves as the line of demarcation that separates one belief from another.

> **Bootlegging the Bible requires someone to consciously compromise the integrity of scriptural clarity in order to gain a profit.**

The moment one is indoctrinated into any belief, they are forced to surrender to the standards of that belief. When the Bible declares that scripture is profitable for doctrine, it is establishing the Bible as being foundational to a disciplined belief. The second benefit is reproof. Reproof brings a level of accountability to one's disciplined belief, by calling every principle of one's belief into account. Reproof is a standard that measures the validity and credibility of all beliefs. The third benefit is correction. Correction is the means by which God actively disciplines His children to keep them from walking in the spirit of error. Finally, instruction in righteousness is a level of discipline that places a high demand upon us not to conform to the world, but rather to be conformed to the image and character of Jesus Christ.

Once again, notice the pattern within this

scripture. At no time in Paul's description of the Word of God to Timothy is there a word given that describes the scriptures with pleasurable terminology. It is because God desires to release us into that which is for our profit, not our pleasure. Carnality is rooted in that which is pleasurable, thus the carnal mind is enmity against God. It is not subject to the law of God and cannot ever be because the carnal mind is programmed for those things that are pleasurable. The carnal mind seeks opportunities to stimulate the body and bring it pleasure, regardless of the cost. However, because the scriptures are profitable for all of these things that pertain to discipline, the Bible becomes a manual in need of revision. Those seeking to revise the scripture are looking to God's Word as a permit for their pleasure. The only way that this can be satisfied is if the scriptures are watered down and compromised. No wonder there are so many people who are not experiencing the fullness of God's power in the way He moved throughout the scriptures.

    God will never compromise His character in order to reach new converts. You will never experience His promise or His power at the expense of His nature! The key to life in the Spirit is when that which is for your profit brings you pleasure.

    The Bible declares in Psalms 119: 47 and 48 "And I will delight myself in thy commandments, which I have loved. My hands also will I lift up unto thy commandments, which I have loved; and I will meditate in thy statutes." Examine how the psalmist views the Word of God. To the psalmist, the Laws of

God are pleasurable, because they are profitable. The psalmist doesn't seem to feel the need to bring God's Word down to his standards. The writer declares that he *loves* God's commandments. Most people view God's commandments as restrictive and prohibitive, yet the psalmist views God's commandments as a source for freedom and delight.

When the Word of God produces an attitude in which one loves it, takes delight in it, and focuses upon it daily, then it will make application pleasurable, not penitential. In contrast, an individual will always feel the need to add on to whatever they are not satisfied with, and take away what they find superfluous or unnecessary.

The key to life in the Spirit is when that which is for your profit brings you pleasure.

However, the psalmist continues to say in that same chapter (verse 129) "Thy testimonies are wonderful: therefore doth my soul keep them." Notice this powerful revelation of the psalmist. When God's testimonies are considered wonderful, *then* will your soul be inclined to keep them!

You will never be motivated to keep God's Word if it isn't wonderful to you. As a result of keeping the testimonies of God that are considered wonderful to the psalmist, then the Word begins to work wonders for the psalmist. Notice the following verse (verse 130) that declares "The entrance of thy words giveth light; it giveth understanding unto the simple." The wonders of the Word are that it illuminates the lives of every individual who adheres to it, which allows the individual to make right choices. The darkness of life's uncertainties is erased and replaced with clarity and vision. Furthermore, the frustrations of ignorance are dismissed and replaced with the power of knowledge. What invaluable resources are produced just by keeping the Word of God!!

Remember after Paul gives the purposes of scripture to Timothy, he gives the outcome. In 2 Timothy 3:17 he tells Timothy, "that the man of God may be perfect, thoroughly furnished unto all good works." Because of the Word of God, every believer can be complete, finished! Next, every believer can be furnished. God wants to both finish us and furnish us through the scriptures, so all we do would be profitable. This can only happen when the Bible is received with the clarity and concision of its original intent. In short, you cannot achieve what God intended for your life if the manual for your life is revised to make life convenient for you. That is the bottom line!

The Bible cannot be rationalized or compromised because you don't like its content. Bootlegging the Bible leaves a believer unfinished and unfurnished. Life will always produce an endless amount of frustrations because you will be rich in potential yet poor in performance. Your destiny (good works) is depending upon you becoming finished. You can't complete anything if you are incomplete. You certainly cannot accomplish anything if you aren't furnished with the resources necessary to accomplish them. There are things you absolutely must have in order to achieve God's purpose for you.

These spiritual things are revealed through the Word of God. That very same source for living is the key to living with the necessary resources. Don't allow yourselves to be taken with every wind and doctrine. No, it isn't necessary to toss out your Bible when you discover after reading this that you have been guided by a bootlegged copy. A bootlegged copy of the Bible isn't based upon whether you have a written translation of Holy Scripture that is filled with inaccuracies.

A bootlegged copy of the Bible rests in how you interpret scripture! It is the way you read, not what you read. It is how you view the scriptures based upon your influences. I don't want you to think that bootlegging the Bible means going out and buying a completely altered version. In other words, bootlegging is a mindset that influences your perception. That is what makes it so dangerous. It is invisible, intangible, and can be overlooked. This perception is what completely alters the scripture.

In order for this to be overcome, you must discard the mindset, not the manual. Your mind must be renewed to the mind of Christ, which ultimately is the deciding factor on judging spiritual matters.

When reading any passage of scripture, or listening to scripture being interpreted or taught, you must ask yourself, "Is Jesus Christ being glorified, or am I?" I found this question to be an underlining theme inherent in all encounters with spiritual matters. There are so many sermons and so much literature out there that look to "inspire" and "uplift," but inspiration must accompany the revelation of Christ. I cannot just look for inspiration and judge if a scripture is being taught or interpreted correctly. I cannot use the "pleasure test" when trying to gauge if I am being fed the Word. I must use the "profit test" if I am to appraise the authenticity of any teaching.

Am I being inspired to exemplify the character of Christ and complete His ministry on earth, or am I being uplifted to just merely feel better about my own life? This is the question that will bring universal translation and interpretation of scripture. This is the question that will produce application of the Bible, not just interpretation. This is the question that will see the Bible become the foundation to all of life's choices and decisions, and a reference guide to every reader. Once this issue settles in the minds of every individual reading scripture, then happiness won't be relative to any and all lifestyles. Jesus' lifestyle and His way of thinking will be the only way of thinking. Any thing other than Christ being glorified is a bootlegged way of thinking.

THE BOOTLEG BREACH

Sitting in a barbershop one Saturday morning, I was approached by a young boy carrying a box filled with compact discs and videotapes. He was selling brand new music from artists whose new releases had been downloaded even before they hit the market. He was also selling videotapes of movies still in theaters. I picked up the non-labeled, coverless videotapes and CDs, firmly placed them against the chest of this young boy who looked no more than 11 years old, and I asked him who gave those to him to sell. He pointed outside and told me that his grandmother did. Angrily, I walked outside and approached an older-looking woman who was sitting impatiently behind the wheel of her car. As I approached the vehicle, I quickly glanced over to the backseat and noticed more boxes of these same items being peddled by this young boy. The woman saw me approaching and asked if I wanted to buy any of her "products." I immediately told her that it wasn't right that she was selling bootlegged copies of artist's materials, and that even worse, she was setting a poor example as a grandmother. I also informed her that she was taking money out of the pockets of those who invested in the material that she now circulated on the black market.

Obviously, she didn't like my response at all. This woman had a few choice words for me and told me that this was how she made her living, and that I had no right to tell her what to do. She angrily exclaimed that she didn't want to hear a sermon or a lecture, and to leave her alone! I walked away from that confrontation understanding that I was infuriated perhaps even more than most people who considered the purchase of these bootlegged copies a bargain. I realized that my indignation was intensified because of my experience in the music industry, and as a recording artist, I experienced the damage of being robbed through unauthorized reproduction of original material. I slowly walked back into the barbershop and sat down defiantly, yet confidently that I stood up for artists everywhere.

One of the barbers commenced to putting in one of the bootlegged copies he had just purchased from that young boy. The tape played with visual distortion and kept playing and kept playing. The entire barbershop stared expectedly at the television monitor, but soon filled with silence from the disappointment of watching only visual distortion. With a look of disgust and frustration, the barber tapped the eject button, grabbed the videocassette angrily, and then tossed it into the garbage can.

The sound of that cassette hitting the bottom of that garbage can seemed to resonate through my spirit. Today I can still hear the loud "thud" reverberating in my ears. This reverberation sparked a revelation. The barber who purchased that bootlegged copy could not take it back to the seller, distributor, or manufacturer because he possessed an illegal copy that wasn't bound to any warranties or guarantees.

The moment he purchased a bootleg copy, he forfeited all rights as a consumer to be protected by any federal and state laws governing the marketplace. The barber had no right to contact the young boy and ask for his money back. If he did, and the young man refused, the barber could not pursue any legal action because of the illegality of his purchase. He could not hold the seller accountable! Bootlegging breaches any and all commitments, contracts, legal rights, obligations, warranties, policies, or covenant agreements. It disqualifies the buyer from having any leverage. So it is when we bootleg the Bible.

By viewing the Word of God with a distorted perception, and looking to revise the scriptures to accommodate our lifestyles, we put ourselves at a disadvantage by voiding all covenant agreements that God made with us in the original manuscript. We lose our "leverage" of being able to hold God at His Word, because it is no longer His Word that we are holding on to.

It is a watered-down, scaled-down version of His Word that we are trying to get God to honor. Remember, God watches over His Word to perform it. This is all predicated upon the Word being His. His promise to perform, accomplish, and fulfill His Word is contingent upon it being His Word, not our own. The moment God's Word is compromised, it becomes a bootlegged copy that breaches all covenants, promises, and agreements that God has made with man.

By viewing the word of God with a distorted perception, and looking to revise the scriptures to accommodate our lifestyles, we put ourselves at a disadvantage by voiding all covenant agreements that God made with us in the original manuscript.

We must hold onto God's Word because that

is our only connection to God's promise to perform what we ask of Him in prayer. Jesus declares in St. John 15:7, "If ye abide in me, and my words abide in you, ye shall ask what ye will, and it shall be done unto you." The key to you getting what you will, is asking what He wills.

What God wills is manifested in you through His words, which then prompts you to ask. In other words, what you are asking for is a result of what is found in God's Word. For it is only His Word that He honors. It isn't you, the one who is doing the asking, although He loves you. It isn't the thing you are asking for, although He wants you to prosper. It is what lies in His Word that evokes God to respond to our prayers. When an individual abides in Him, they are living daily according to God's Word. They are governing their lives according to His Word, daily. That is abiding in Him.

I want you to see how bootlegging breaches that covenant promise that God makes in St. John 15. When His words are not abiding in you, and you are not abiding in His words, then you will experience what James 4:2 describes as "having not because you ask not. You ask and receive not, because you ask amiss, that you may consume it upon your lust (pleasures)." There goes that word again, pleasures!

No longer is the individual seeking what is for their profit, but rather what is for their pleasure. This is powerful! The results found in James are contradistinctive to the results found in John.

Notice that the individual in James is asking

amiss. They are praying selfishly and greedily based upon their own lusts. We can deduce that this individual isn't abiding in God's Word or God's Word abiding in them. Although they may even be praying God's promises, their motives for receiving these promises are wrong, which breaches the promise that God makes to give them what they ask for. Therefore, bootlegging is done by consciously compromising the integrity of scriptural clarity in order to gain a profit. God cannot reward us when our motives are selfish, and we are only out for personal gain. This contradicts God's character. The Word without compromise is the only thing that can change our motives to unselfish, pure intentions. Now God's Divine Will can be accomplished primarily because His words are abiding in the heart.

THE BONDAGE OF BOOTLEGGING

One of the greatest passages of scripture is found in St. John 8: 31–32. It is here where the Bible tells us that Jesus said to those Jews which believed on Him. "If you continue in my word, then are you my disciples indeed . . ." Jesus always admonished His disciples and everyone else who believed on Him to do what was profitable for their continual development. He never endorsed any activity that merely appeased the moment and appealed to the masses. Jesus understood that life in the Word was the only way in which direct connection to God's power and promises would continue. Therefore, it was necessary to persist in a lifestyle that circled around the precepts of Christ, following His commandments and abiding in His teachings. There could be no compromises or deviations along the way. Discipleship was proven when this occurred.

The word disciple also means "disciplined one". Isn't that the same thing that Paul establishes with Timothy in 2 Timothy 3:16? "All scripture is given by inspiration of God and is profitable for doctrine, reproof, correction, and instruction in righteousness." All of these together will produce a disciplined one (disciple) who will become finished and furnished unto all good works. Jesus sought to make disciplined men out of mere men. His desire for us is that we have a disciplined mind and live a disciplined life.

How many poor decisions could we have avoided if only we were disciplined to doing the right thing? How many wrongdoings could have been averted if we were disciplined in not following after our flesh?

The truth is, when someone sins and breaks God's laws, it is because they haven't disciplined themselves to doing what is right, regardless of what feels right. Holiness doesn't rest in the absence of temptation. It is in the discipline not to yield to temptation. This extends far beyond good and evil, right and wrong. It goes into the heart of profitable and unprofitable, faithful and unfaithful stewardship. This is whether you are trying to lay aside every weight, or trying to lose weight. Discipline is the key to a healthy lifestyle, a successful Christian walk, and a debt-free life. Unfortunately, Christians are some of the most undisciplined people in the earth. This reflects poorly upon the One we are representing. Jesus tells us in St. John 8:31 "If ye continue in my word, then are ye my disciples indeed;"

> **The only truth that frees a man is the truth he knows.**

Life in the Word validates our profession. Notice why. The next verse is the key: (verse 32) " . . . and you shall know the truth . . ." Notice that continuing in His Word is the only way to know the truth. Spending time consistently in Christ's words ensures that one is personally acquainted and intimate with truth. A disciplined life is a life that results from knowing the truth, and knowing the truth is a result of spending life abiding in truth. This knowledge of the truth will be characterized in a disciplined life. The decisions you make will be profitable according to the truth that you know. Then Jesus says something powerful. He says, "And the truth shall make you free." This verse is always quoted in part. We have said, "The truth shall make you free." That is incorrect.

The only truth that frees a man is the truth he knows! You can't be freed by a truth you are unfamiliar with, and you cannot become familiar with a truth that you don't abide in. It is that simple! Therefore, ignorance to the truth is bondage, and as long as you don't know the truth, you are imprisoned to life's cycles. It then becomes impossible to discipline one's life because there is no standard by which to gauge right or wrong, profitable or unprofitable, good or evil. Knowing the truth creates an internal, moral compass that navigates your way throughout all of life's journeys.

What is Truth?

This question has reverberated throughout the ages. From the time Pilate asked Jesus this before sentencing Him to be crucified, to this present day in which churches are warring over doctrinal and denominational differences, the question remains, "What is truth?" It seems that you can find truth hiding under every rock, lying in every alley, filtering through the literature of every religion, circulating throughout every media outlet, and generating from every theorist, psychologist, and scientist.

Everyone seems to have cornered the market on the *truth*. With each one of these entities competing and vying for the undisputed crown of "Possessor of Truth," it makes knowing the truth more difficult than ever before. The reality is that the truth we do know is a hodgepodge of influences from many of these sources. I have discovered that knowing the truth is becoming increasingly more difficult with the passing of each generation, because every generation surrenders or compromises what was once embraced as truth in order to be relevant in the times in which they live.

In St. John 18:37, Pilate heard Jesus say, "To

this end was I born, and for this cause came I into the world, that I should bear witness unto the truth. Every one that is of the truth heareth my voice." Jesus dared to establish Himself as being the voice of truth. To Pilate, this must have sounded arrogant and absurd. Pilate himself must have grown cynical and wearied of hearing religious and political figures professing to know the real truth.

I am sure that in Pilate's day, he was exposed to so many beliefs from his own pagan influence, as well as all of the beliefs from the Jewish culture. For after all, if Jesus Himself was the truth who claimed to be the King of the Jews, then why would the Jews themselves call Him a mocker and a blasphemer?

So to Pilate, even the Jews had trouble knowing what was considered truth. Therefore, in response to Jesus' claim, Pilate's words were laced with skepticism and cynicism. Thus, he didn't wait for a response from Jesus when asking this question. I believe it wasn't a question posed to be answered, but rather a cynical remark in the form of an inquisition. It seemed as if Pilate doubted that there was such a thing as truth, with so many beliefs prevalent in his day. So this question continues to echo throughout the annals of time and the halls of our most revered institutions. And that is, "What is truth?"

Truths can be found in so many places. However, the absolute truth can only be found in one place—in the Word of God that declares "I am the way, the truth, and the life: no man cometh unto the Father, but by me." (St. John 14:6) It is this truth that causes controversy. It is this truth that causes division. It is this truth that divides a nation, disturbs the political process, disrupts the educational institutions, and disassembles the legal system. This is absolute truth, because it draws a line in the sand.

Everyone can claim to know a god, to worship a god, to kneel to a higher power, and that brings little controversy outside of atheistic grievances. However, to declare that Jesus is Lord declares a particular group of people as being the possessor of real truth, and it denounces any other form of religion.

Jesus is the only way to the Heavenly Father! There is no other way to God except through His Son, Jesus Christ. Bootlegging this truth is found in diminishing Jesus' deity, dismissing His contributions to our redemption, and accepting all faiths for the purposes of unity. Unity must be the heartbeat of any people, but not at the irregular heartbeat of compromise.

Once Jesus is no longer "the" way, but "a" way, once Jesus Christ is no longer "the" truth, but "a" truth, once Jesus Christ is no longer "the" life, but "another" way to life, then the truth has just been bootlegged. From there, it becomes impossible to "know the truth," because that would be forfeited when embracing other truths, ways, and means to life. You absolutely cannot know the truth without knowing Jesus Christ, for He is truth. The Bible clearly declares, "If the Son therefore shall make you free, ye shall be free indeed." (St. John 8:36)

Notice that Jesus declares this after He tells

them that they shall know the truth and the truth shall make them free. The verses before verse 36 shed even greater light on the bondage of not knowing the truth. The people answered him, "We are of Abraham's seed, and were never in bondage to any man: how say you, you shall be made free?" They were confused as to what Jesus really meant. They considered bondage as literal slavery that would result in the inability to exercise any freedom or liberty, which they proclaimed in their religious arrogance. Jesus however was speaking of a far greater slavery. He was speaking of a bondage that could never be lifted with a political, religious, military, or social uprising. He was speaking of a bondage that took more than weapons and political reforms to break. He was speaking of the bondage of sin. When one commits it, one is considered a servant to it.

    The fact was, their sins brought desolation and death, and although faced with the consequences of their actions, they were powerless to stop it. This, to Jesus, was bondage. The cause of this was that their sins separated them from God and from their covenant with God. So although they were Abraham's seed, they were not walking in Abraham's covenant of promise. This was a covenant that was established upon relationship with the Father. Obedience was the connector to the covenant.

    Without a relationship with God, there is no willingness for obedience, which nullifies any covenant agreement!! Relationship cuts the covenant; obedience confirms it! Abraham's seed had breeched the covenant agreement because they walked away from God and began a cycle of disobedience called sin. Jesus establishes Himself as the truth because only He is the way to God, therefore only He could reconcile the world back to the Father.

Jesus said it best in St. John 10:1 when He declares, "He that enters not by the door into the sheepfold, but climbs up some other way, the same is a thief and a robber." Later in that same chapter, Jesus confirms Himself to be the door of the sheep. He is the way, the truth, and the life. Anyone who attempts to get into God's awesome promises of salvation and eternal life any other way is a thief and a robber.

Just like a bootlegger, they are accessing the way illegally and must be considered thieves and robbers. Notice that Jesus says, " . . . but climbs up some other way . . ." He calls them thieves and robbers. They are not considered thieves and robbers because they took something.

As a matter of fact, the scriptures don't even mention anything being taken, yet they are declared to be perpetrators of theft and robbery. The crime is the unlawful entry, not the thievery of any items. It is the conscious effort of trying to avoid the truth in Jesus Christ, by substituting Him for another way. This substitution will never be the truth. This access will never be the way. This replacement will never be the life. It will only be a bootlegged personality perpetrating as a means to God's promises. Make no mistake about it, Jesus is the truth. That is why His

Name stirs up controversy. That is why His Name is followed by contempt and animosity, and all of those who are followers of Christ are constantly being targeted in the media and throughout the entire world. Christians are some of the most hated people around the world, because Christians dare claim to have the truth. To the world, this claim is not only arrogant, but offensive!

Chapter 2

CHRISTIANITY IN CRISIS

There are those who stand daily upon the frontlines fighting for our religious freedoms. Churches all across America are urging their members to pray for local, state, and federal government officials. There has never before in the history of this country been such widespread involvement from churches in the political process. It is because Supreme Court rulings and activist groups are turning the tide in America by seeking to create a liberal society that is godless and antireligious. Our religious freedoms are under fire, and the attack is relentless. Every news agency across this country that directly influences what is reported, as well as television networks that decide the types of programming that you watch, are ran by liberals whose agenda is to filter in filth and flush out faith. Make no mistake about it; their agenda is clear. Create an environment that is hostile toward Christianity by perverting the tenets of our faith and distorting the message of the Bible. Meanwhile, display alternative lifestyles as not only acceptable but normal, and qualify anyone who opposes these lifestyles as a bigot and a hatemonger. With legislation being passed that conflict with Christianity, this would seem to be the cause for Christianity being in a crisis.

    I would dare say that the greatest enemy to our Christianity isn't the political system, the judicial system, activist groups, or the media. The reason that Christianity is in a crisis is because of the state of the church. The climate of the church is one of compromise, in which professed Christians are serving a more modern, tolerant god whom they have manufactured from worldly influences. Like the children of Israel at the foot of Mt. Sinai investing together their gold in which to make a golden calf that they could worship and serve, professed believers are investing their ideologies and philosophies into a "melting pot" of theology and have created their own "god" to which they bow. This modern-day, golden calf is nothing more than a black-market god that authorizes and endorses lifestyles and views that are contrary to the laws given by our Heavenly Father as revealed in Holy Scripture!

    This has resulted in professed Christians doing more to diminish the influence of Christianity upon this society than any Supreme Court ruling or any piece of political legislation. These professing Christians have done more to refute the authority of Holy Scriptures than any slanted documentary portrayed by the media. They have done more to challenge the existence of an eternal Creator than any atheistic group. It has been the ones who have professed faith in God that have damaged the integrity of the faith with their hypocrisy. The result is Christianity in crisis.

This crisis is because of individuals not serving the God of the Bible, but a black market god who is more than willing to accept any lifestyle. Don't get me wrong, we need people on the frontlines to defend our religious freedoms. We need voices in the political arena who will challenge legislation that threaten to cast a liberal shadow over the entire United States of America. We need faces on the television screen that will represent what is in the best moral interest to our society. However, we need leaders in our churches who will reestablish God to be the God of the Bible. We need leaders who are not afraid of political and social fallout because they dare stand up and declare right and wrong.

Christianity is crying out for leaders who are not trying to become political figures seeking to win popularity polls. Christianity is crying out for leaders who are willing to lose tithe-paying members, gifted leaders, and celebrity guests, because they decry the acceptance of an open and free lifestyle. Christianity is longing for the days when people won't mind being different, and when they aren't trying to fit into a politically correct system. Christianity is giving a clarion call for professed believers to become a people whose God is the Lord!

Michael Lowery

MATERIALISM AND COMMERCIALISM

There are a few key elements that are also contributing factors to Christianity being in a crisis. These agents have driven the black market and have caused the value of true Christianity to depreciate. Never before has there been such a major influence of materialism and commercialism than today. It is because we are in a market-driven society, and the saints have assimilated to the world's mindset.

The Bible declares in Romans 12:1–2, "I beseech you therefore brethren by the mercies of God that you would present your bodies a living sacrifice, holy, acceptable unto God which is your reasonable service. And be not conformed to this world, but be ye transformed by the renewing of your mind that you may prove what is that good, acceptable, and perfect will of God." Paul admonishes that we not be conditioned or fashioned by the influences of the world. He encourages us to be changed by changing the way we think. World conformity doesn't just rest in copying the sinfulness of the world, but copying the world's mentality and methods. What many in the church have always believed is that their greatest nemesis is the world's sinfulness. As we see in St. Matthew Chapter 4, one of the greatest tests of Jesus' ministry was regarding materialism. The devil offered Jesus all the kingdoms of the world and the glory of them.

The devil offered Jesus *things*. That was one of the three temptations in the wilderness that Jesus encountered. Today one of the greatest tests of the church by the devil rests in materialism. Worldliness is based upon materialism, not just sinful behaviors. The society in which we live is materialistic, driven by market-influenced ideologies and schemes.

People come into the church with this worldly mindset, and they can only identify with spiritual matters if they are delivered through marketing techniques and philosophies. It is virtually impossible not to have this mindset because we are besieged with commercials, infomercials, advertisements, and solicitations. Everyone is competing for our dollar, and because we have been conditioned to believe that "the customer is always right," we have assumed an arrogance that causes us to be "goods-and-services oriented."

Now we look for the church that offers us the most service for our tithe! We expect the church to have a ministry for everyone in the family, including the family pet, and God forbid if that ministry has just begun, then we will seek another, more "established" church.

There must be conferences for women, meetings for men, ministry for the children at every age level, ministry for the couples, singles, divorcees, premarital ministry, camps, clubs, summer programs, child care, etc. All of these things must be in place *before* we join. The pastor becomes discouraged because he keeps losing members to the church down the street that is offering all of these goods and services, so he decides to "compete" by stretching an already overburdened staff to filling these roles. Even worse, he will reduce himself to becoming a spiritual booster who commits pulpit piracy by "lifting" sermons, ministry styles, and vision statements in an attempt to copy the methods of successful ministries. Instead of being mentored or fathered by anointed leaders, these individuals covet the methods and mannerisms of successful leaders by repeaching the sermons of others, repeating prophecies, or re-enacting the move of God manifested in other ministries. These leaders begin to operate outside of the areas of their grace and gifting, and that local assembly is then left without a specific Word for the life of their ministry. It then begins to buckle under the unjust weight of another ministry's Divine Calling. Consequently, these smaller ministries, instead of experiencing an explosion in growth they so desperately seek, wind up witnessing an implosion.

Now we look for the church that offers us the most service for our tithe.

Thus the big churches become even bigger because they have all this to offer and the smaller churches get smaller because they do not. The problem isn't in being willing to offer these services to the congregation, but in the thinking of individuals who judge if a church is right for them based upon all of these components being in place. Just as in the world, where the consumer is becoming more sophisticated and demanding with his dollar, so it is in the church. What drives people to think with this kind of mindset? It is because commercialism influences their thinking, which is centered upon materialism. Materialism is at the heart of commercialism. It is what drives the market, and truthfully, it is what drives the black market.

One would think that a person would see the obvious difference between a church and the world. One would think that an individual would simply discard that way of thinking when they arrive at church. However, changing a way of thinking isn't just that simple. That's why Romans 12:2 tells us that we are transformed by the renewing of our minds. This means that we experience a metamorphosis as we change the way we think. It takes an extended period of time as well as an ongoing renewing in order for someone's thinking to change. Therefore, people bring the unregenerate mind to the church and begin to see spiritual work from a worldly viewpoint.

So if materialism is at the heart of commercialism, then what can a person possibly acquire from the church that would perpetuate this mindset? When a person is materialistic, it isn't the acquisition that brings the fulfillment or satisfaction. A materialistic individual uses things as a tool to find importance and self-worth in life. They unfortunately have defined their life based upon the things that they have, but this is an elusive endeavor that breeds dissatisfaction and disappointment because things can never bring fulfillment or contentment. They continue to obsess over trivial, material matters that cannot ever be satisfied.

Notice Satan in his attempts to lure Jesus into

temptation with the last of the three temptations that is recorded in St. Matthew 4:9. He said to Jesus, "All these things will I give thee, if thou will fall down and worship me." Satan has ownership of things, for he is the prince of this material world. Things are obviously an influential part of his kingdom, but the Bible is implying that things aren't his most sought after commodity. The devil wants to be worshipped. He wants to be praised. He wants to be exalted like God. Notice what this verse suggests.

Although Satan has the glory of the kingdoms of this world along with the riches, he is willing to exchange his material possessions for worship! He is willing to forfeit kingdoms for worth-ship! He is seeking worth and importance and is using the lure of materialism to get it. He is revealing that materialism is the tool to attempt to acquire worth and importance.

Commercialism then becomes a marketing strategy that advertises opportunities to receive self-worth and importance! It is a campaign to reward the potential customer with goods and services that would make them feel like they are somebody! This strategy unfortunately has permeated the church, and ministries are subjecting themselves to commercialism in order to grow a church.

Once commercialism becomes the attitude of the local assembly, it will pervert ministry into an all-inclusive benefit package designed to cater to the needs of every individual. This not only hinders the Body of Christ universally, but it produces a quagmire of compromise that will result in covert competition between local assemblies that drives the universal body out of Kingdom business.

> **Unfortunately, true servants in the house of the Lord are quickly becoming an endangered species. The cause is consumerism.**

Consumerism

I stood in an aisle at the neighborhood Wal-Mart store, looking for cleaning items. As I made my way down the aisle, I noticed a small puddle of liquid had apparently spilled from an item that toppled from the shelf. I stepped over that dangerous spill and continued making my way to the items that I came to purchase. The moment I approached the checkout counter, I heard a loud voice over the intercom dispatching a worker to that same particular aisle in order to clean up that spill.

As I looked back over that incident, I realized that I did what many attendants in church do every church service. I came to the store as a customer; therefore, my only mentality was to make a purchase. I was thinking like a consumer who concluded that any spills were not my responsibility. I was thinking like a consumer who felt that any work or labor was a duty assigned to those people who were employed by that company. In other words, it was always someone else's job! How many times do pastors or church leaders become frustrated because they cannot find people who are willing to serve? Unfortunately, true servants in the house of the Lord are quickly becoming an endangered species. The cause is consumerism. People come in to church thinking like consumers who are only there to receive a blessing. People think as I thought that day at the Wal-Mart store.

The spill was somebody else's problem. The work to be performed was the responsibility of somebody else. Think about it! When was the last time you saw a customer moving a box that was in the middle of the aisle, picking up a can that fell out of place, or mopping the floor from a spill that occurred? You probably haven't! It is because we walk into a place of business knowing our role.

Our role is to be a consumer! That is why it is so easy to step over spills, walk around work needing to be completed, or disregard disturbances altogether. People generally seek places of worship with ministries already in place to satisfy their every need. It is easier to join something that is already set up and in place than to partner into something that requires you to make a great investment. I have heard people say that they don't want to be a part of building something; they would rather have things already in place. How ignorant is that thinking? Do they not realize that the greatest dividends are the results of the greatest investments? Those who take the greatest risks are those who receive the greatest rewards!

There is always a great disparity between the amount of people going to the church, and the amount of people really carrying the church. Usually, the disproportion is staggering in the number of people who faithfully tithe and those who only tip occasionally, not to mention the fact that more things are done by a few rather than the majority.

Churches are top-heavy with blessing seekers and starving from lack of servants. Once again, it is the spirit of consumerism that has pushed the Body of Christ to a place of imbalance.

People generally come to church looking to be inspired, seeking to be blessed, and longing to be encouraged, rather than seeking instruction from God regarding the role they are to play in the advancement of that local body. Believe it or not, this mentality affects our positions with the church, our postures in the church, and our perceptions of the church. Those are the three components that affect everything we do in the church, and they are all influenced directly by consumerism.

A person who thinks like a consumer perceives the church as a place from which they get blessings. They posture themselves in the church as people whose hands are out to receive. They position themselves with the church as people who analyze and criticize what is and what isn't being done, rather than seeking how they can make things run better. How we perceive something directly influences how we perform with it, because perception determines performance. The way you view a thing will directly control how you treat it. When people perceive the church to be a place to take rather than to invest, to get rather than give, to be served rather than to serve, it will cause their performance in church to be self-motivated.

Our posture within the church says a lot about our thinking concerning it. Often we show very little concern for things outside of our own needs. Therefore, individuals can only relate to God on an "I need" basis, wherein He becomes our supplier rather than our Lord. In order for the black market to flourish, there must be a supplier. Someone must furnish and manufacture the items to sell for this illegal system of trade.

While God will not descend to our level and become some cosmic errand boy, we continue to posture ourselves like He is our supplier only, while completely disregarding His laws and truths. We desperately want God to supply our needs, to manufacture our wants, and to stockpile our desires. One's position within the church is then reduced to being a consumer only, and servitude is always someone else's job. If we finally decide to serve in ministry, something is expected in return.

We must be recognized for "services rendered," and we supply God with our invoice called a prayer request, demanding that He remit payment in the form of a miracle. How unfortunate and unfair is this perception, posture, and position because churches are left in wanting.

We must be recognized for "services rendered," and we supply God with our invoice called a prayer

request, demanding that He remit payment in the form of a miracle.

The "How-to" Church

The secular influence of today's culture upon the twenty-first-century church is overwhelming, and this isn't an exaggerated fact. Once again, Romans 12:2 declares that we "Be not conformed to this world . . ." Our ideologies, methods, and philosophies cannot be based upon a worldly viewpoint. If we are not careful, we will find ourselves marrying methods from this secular culture with spiritual principles and trying to get them to reproduce blessings for those who claim to really need them. We will begin building sermons and messages based upon a "how-to" approach. The churches of America are quickly becoming the "how-to" industrial leaders in today's black marketplace. Think about how many magazines and television programs there are circulating that reveal steps to achieving certain results.

Today's world is filled with do-it-yourself programs, how-to tapes and books, as well as secular speakers promoting methods. Major dollars are made to promote methods because they are advertised as simple, easy, and affordable ways of obtaining the desired results. This practical approach to successes in life is very attractive even to the most fundamentally challenged individual. The problem with the "how-to" method (which includes "steps to, ways to, and guides to") is that it produces a church with a lot of outlines and no unction.

The church universally is missing the one component that caused it to explode in the first century, and that is the unction of the Holy Spirit. It seems as though the anointing of God is being replaced with outlines and procedures. People are becoming more pragmatic and regimented in their theological approach to God and less inclined to move under the inspiration of an intelligible yet invisible being called the Spirit of God. The charismatic movement within the church has been squelched by the revolutionary march of the pragmatists! More spiritual leaders are selling methods rather than teaching members to walk after the Spirit.

The problem with the "how-to" method is that it produces a church with a lot of outlines and no unction.

To our culture, it must be practical if it is to be relevant. Don't get me wrong. I do encourage messages that can be understood and truths that are presented in such a way that they are considered practical, but not to the place where they dismiss faith altogether. There must be left to the hearers a place of total dependency upon God's Spirit. They must know that outside of God's guidance they are unable to accomplish their purposes in life.

Every believer must know that his walk with the Lord will include intangibles and the unexpected. Successes will be determined by their willingness to believe God with the things they cannot understand.

There are some things we cannot achieve through the "how-to" method. There are some things that will be achieved in life that cannot be determined by a pre-determined amount of steps. We are not the master controller of our own lives; our steps are ordered of the Lord. The anointing of the Holy Spirit is what empowers us to get wealth and prosperity, to overcome sadness and depression, and to break the curses of generations before us. Once the Body of Christ returns back to the days when it thrived on unction rather than outlines, it will once again be the most powerful living organism known to man.

Chapter 3

A "House of Prayer" or a "Den of Thieves"

In St. Matthew 21:12, the Bible declares, "And Jesus went into the temple of God, and cast out all them that sold and bought in the temple, and overthrew the tables of the moneychangers, and the seats of them that sold doves, (v 13) and said unto them, 'It is written, My house shall be called the house of prayer, but you have made it a den of thieves.'" No greater example given to us in scripture illustrates the black market more than the events that occurred within this passage. For within this act of cleansing the temple, Jesus exposes the state of the temple during His ministry and the state of the church in this twenty-first century. Notice that the activity that was taking place in this text openly defiled God's house, because it blatantly defied God's laws. Therefore, Jesus' response and subsequent purging of the temple was warranted.

First of all, let's examine verse 13. Verse 13

reveals the reason for Jesus' indignation. This verse sheds greater light on the way God views His house.

God always intended for His house to be a House of Prayer. Jesus said emphatically, "It is written, my house shall be called the house of prayer . . ." This statement establishes God's divine purpose for the temple. God wants His house dedicated for the prayers of His people. 2 Chronicles 6:19 declares, "Have respect therefore to the prayer of thy servant, and to his supplication, O Lord my God, to hearken unto the cry and the prayer which thy servant prays before thee: (v20) That your eyes may be open upon this house day and night, upon the place whereof thou hast said that thou would put thy name there; to hearken unto the prayer which thy servant prays towards this place."

It was King Solomon's desire that the temple of God fulfill its purpose, which was to be a House of Prayer. He believed that if there was a place on earth set aside for the sole purpose of communicating with God, then God would honor every petition made in that place . As a matter of fact, King Solomon desired that God's eyes would remain upon the place wherein His Name dwelled, to listen to the words of the faithful and to supply their needs.

It is interesting that King Solomon was not beckoning for God's eyes to roam throughout every place watching every individual, but rather that God's eyes would remain over His house, to answer every prayer made toward that place. That's the reason for his determination to build God a house that had beauty and splendor beyond anything imaginable. King Solomon, with all of his wisdom, must have known something that we have yet to grasp.

God's house should represent and resemble where He dwells. God's house should be indicative of where God exists. God's house should reflect His glorious presence, which King Solomon believed would provoke God's response. This was Solomon's prayer request in Chapter 6. Notice that King Solomon did not wait for the answer before he set his heart to building this temple. As a matter of fact, King Solomon built the House of the Lord *believing* that God would hear his prayer and choose that house. In 2 Chronicles 7:11, it declares, "Thus Solomon finished the house of the Lord, and the king's house: and all that came into Solomon's heart to make in the house of the Lord, and in his own house, he prosperously effected." Verse 12 then says, "And the Lord appeared to Solomon by night, and said unto him, I have heard thy prayer, and have chosen this place to myself for a house of sacrifice." Notice how God answered King Solomon after the temple was completed! He chose the place *after* King Solomon made such a great investment.

God's house should represent and resemble where He dwells.

Most of us would wait until after we were sure that God would accept something that required great sacrifice before we made the sacrifice. However, by King Solomon building the temple, not entirely certain if God would choose it for His Name to dwell there, he must have been willing to suffer a great loss if his sacrificial offering was rejected. Furthermore, most of us would show God the architectural renderings before we built it in order to get approval. Because, after all, consider the money, time, and labor that went into such a great undertaking.

Surely we would wait until the plans were approved! I believe that was the reason why this temple was chosen. It wasn't chosen because of the splendor, but it was chosen because of the sacrifice. It was chosen because of King Solomon's willingness to suffer great loss for the purposes of God's glory being revealed. Therefore, we must conclude that the House of the Lord is the House of Prayer because it is a house of great sacrifice. It is dedicated and designed out of selflessness not selfishness. God chose that temple to be a place for Him because of the great sacrifice that King Solomon made, just as God chose the church as a place for Himself because of the great sacrifice that Jesus made.

When Jesus walked into the temple in St. Matthew 21, He saw that the temple had been desecrated by greed and selfishness, when it originally was dedicated by glory and selflessness. People were operating in a mode of taking from the temple, looking to see how much they could get out of the temple, rather than what they could bring to the temple. It immediately lost its power because it lost its purpose. It lost its purity because it lost its purpose. It lost its praise because it lost its purpose.

No longer did the House of God exist according to why God chose it. It had become an underworld of black market scam artists who were hustling to make money. How far have we strayed from God's original intent! The temple was never meant to be turned into just another marketplace where secular transactions abound. Furthermore, the temple was never purposed to be a center for social and political activities. God's house should be a place where the cries of His people can be heard.

The church of today must reflect God's original intent for His temple. In King Solomon's day, the temple was chosen solely for prayer, but out of a spirit of sacrifice. It was King Solomon's willingness to invest in the finest of fixtures and vessels in order to build God a house that was indicative of His Splendor, when there was the possibility of him losing out on his investment. God honors sacrifice! In return, He promised to hearken unto the prayers that were made within the place of that sacrifice and would call it a house of sacrifice!

The church of today must reflect God's original intent for His temple.

"IF MY PEOPLE"

One of the most used and often quoted verses in the Bible is found in 2 Chronicles 7:14. "If my people, which are called by my name, shall humble themselves and pray, and seek my face, and turn from their wicked ways; then will I hear from heaven, and will forgive their sin, and will heal their land." This is readily quoted because of the promises that God made. While we are living in a time of great darkness and disease, we embrace the hope that if we meet the conditions laid out for us in this verse, God will perform as He promised. As often as this scripture is quoted, it isn't recited within its proper context. If you notice earlier in this same chapter, God had just answered King Solomon regarding a prayer that he had prayed concerning God receiving the house that he built as the House of Prayer.

  King Solomon made a great investment before receiving an answer that God would sanctify this beautiful temple to establish His Name there. God honored King Solomon's sacrifice and told him that He chose that temple to be His house of prayer and sacrifice. Then God revealed to King Solomon a powerful revelation concerning the cause behind the circumstances that would befall the children of Israel.

  If there was a severe drought, locusts devouring the land, or even pestilence among the people, it would be because He permitted it. God revealed that He would cause these circumstances in the hope that they would perhaps drive Israel to her knees and cry out to Him. Then after He established the cause for their crisis, He laid out the conditions for their cure. While in that period, it was God who sought communion with His people in the place He had chosen, where His Name was revered and His glory revealed. As a matter of fact, verse 14 is incomplete! God continued to answer King Solomon, "Now my eyes shall be open, and my ears attentive to the prayer that is made in this place.

For now have I chosen and sanctified this house that my name may be there for ever: and my eyes and my heart shall be there perpetually." (verses 15 & 16) God had just revealed the zeal of His house. He answered King Solomon's prayers concerning the temple being the House of God and established it as being the House of Prayer. God was talking about hearing the prayers of His people called by His Name, in the place where His Name dwelled.

Therefore, 2 Chronicles 7:14, although isolated, cannot be fulfilled apart from the House of Prayer. The prayers that are being made in verse 14 are being made in the House of Prayer, because that is what God is establishing.

In other words, as long as the House of God isn't the House of Prayer, His people cannot have their prayers heard from heaven, their sins forgiven, or their land healed, because this promise was based upon the condition of the House of the Lord. That is why God said in the next verse that His eyes shall be open and His ears attentive to the prayers made in the House of Prayer. How often does the church disregard what is taking place in God's house, but want God to bring blessings upon their house? God is very zealous concerning the condition of His house. In the gospel of St. John 2:17, the disciples remembered that it was written, "The zeal of thy house hath eaten me up." The disciples were trying to understand the level of Jesus' indignation. They were trying to grasp why the Savior exhibited such anger over the activities in the temple.

For it is in the gospel of John that records Jesus making a "scourge" of small cords, driving them out of the temple, along with the sheep and the oxen, pouring out the monies from their bags, and overthrowing their tables. This perhaps was the most violent display of Jesus' character that they had ever witnessed, and I am sure the degree of Jesus' anger took them by surprise. So when trying to understand the reason for such a violent outburst, they remembered the scripture in Psalms 69:9 that declares, "For the zeal of thy house hath eaten me up; and the reproaches of them that reproached thee are fallen upon me." Jesus was outraged by what He saw, so much so that God's original purpose became a consuming fire within Him.

For as long as the House of Prayer was a den of thieves, it was a house with no power.

This ignited a passion to purge out anything and everything that defied God's purpose and plan. This reproach kindled such a righteous indignation within Jesus, for it offended Him personally. Remember that the purpose for the House of Prayer was so that the people who were called by God's Name could pray, seek His face, and turn from their wicked ways. God wanted to forgive their sins and heal their land.

God wanted to perform miracles that would lead to their healing from any and all diseases. God wants our land healed. God desires for our lives to be changed. That's why in Matthew's gospel, after the House of the Lord was purified, it became a House of Power. The Bible declares that the blind and the lame came to Him in the temple, and He healed them. He healed them in the place where His Name dwelled. That's what He promised to do in 2 Chronicles, and here we see this promise being performed. Notice that Jesus didn't heal them until He purged the house.

For as long as the House of Prayer was a den of thieves, it was a house with no power. He couldn't heal in the temple until the house became a House of Prayer, and it couldn't become that until it was purified.

Just as in 2 Chronicles, God couldn't forgive sins and heal the land until His people turned from their wicked ways. When His people who are called by His Name live and worship in a den of thieves, they continue to live with the same diseases and wicked ways, unable to walk in deliverance because they lack access to the power in which to do it. That's what made Jesus drive out the thieves. As long as they were operating in the temple, the blind would still be unable to see, the lame unable to walk, and sin would remain.

How little regard do we have for the House of Prayer, not realizing that the condition of God's house is directly related to our own physical, emotional, and spiritual condition? We believe that 2 Chronicles 7:14 can be accomplished independent of God's house, and that simply is not true. If you look at the types of activities taking place within the churches of the twenty-first century, you will find that prayer is the least one occurring. Yet Jesus said, "My house shall be called the house of prayer." As a matter of fact, most prayer meetings are seldom held and poorly attended.

It is because the church has lost focus on what it is called to be. You will find churches hosting concerts, theatrical performances, dances, political meetings, banquets, etc. However, when it comes to prayer, people stay away. How could we minor in the most essential, yet major in the least? How could we emphasize what is least important, yet de-emphasize what is the most important? While we are operating at an imbalance, the land is parched from a lack of rain, pestilence (disease) is plaguing our world, and the locusts are devouring our land. Why is it so difficult to get believers to gather together to pray, yet so easy to gather together for a musical or concert? It is because prayer not only works, but prayer takes work! The entertainment factor is completely eliminated. The reason why prayer is the forgotten essential in our Christian walk, and why people support every other function within the church other than prayer, is because it takes effort to pray fervently and effectually.

One must be completely involved, and willing to push one's own feelings aside in order to intercede. Prayer and intercession are quite possibly the most selfless acts that one could commit to. The House of God can never be a House of Prayer, but rather a den of thieves, as long as people are self-centered and self-motivated.

The Livestock Market

In St. Matthew 3:16, Matthew depicts Jesus' ascension out of the Jordan, immediately upon being baptized of John. He descriptively details Christ being met with the heavens opening unto Him. Jesus is then affirmed by the voice of His Father declaring, "This is my beloved Son, in whom I am well pleased." Then one of the most poignant descriptions throughout all of scripture is revealed in this text, and that is the description of the Holy Spirit.

The Holy Spirit is described as descending like a dove, and lighting upon Jesus. In St. Luke 2:22, Luke records this same experience in which the Holy Spirit "descended in a bodily shape like a dove upon Him."

In St. Mark 1:10, Mark describes the Spirit "like a dove descending upon him." Three of the four gospel writers all detail this experience of Jesus' anointing, with the Holy Spirit descending like a dove upon Him. In my mind's eye, I visualize an anointing that is both bold and beautiful, an anointing that is both honorable and humbling. The picture I get of the Holy Spirit's anointing of Jesus is that of power and purity, intensity and intimacy. That is the scene at the shore of the Jordan River.

All three of these gospel writers record the Holy Spirit's tangible anointing as a dove descending upon Jesus. The dove is the perfect symbol and representation of the Holy Spirit, as the sheep is of the saint. However, when Jesus enters into the temple in St. Matthew 21:12, we see a contrasting depiction of the dove. In St. Matthew 3:16, the dove is being sent. In St. Matthew 21:12, the dove is being sold.

When Jesus ascends out of the Jordan, the dove as the Holy Spirit is ministering unto Him. When Jesus enters into the temple, the dove as the Holy Spirit is being merchandised and marketed.

The picture of the Holy Spirit as the dove after Jesus' baptism is of one flying freely, descending, and sitting upon Him. In the temple, the Holy Spirit as the dove is bound and controlled, unable to fly freely, destitute and sitting in a cage.

The results of thievery in the temple couldn't be farther from God's original intent! There are those in ministry who are trying to black market the anointing, merchandising it to its highest bid, just so that they can profit. These are scam artists who want to get rich by prostituting the gift of the Holy Spirit through manipulation. They offer for a price what Jesus gave freely. How many times do we see it on television, hear it on the radio, or witness it firsthand? They are merely thieves in the temple selling doves, looking to offer God's anointing for something in return.

Before you send money to another television ministry or financially support another outreach ministry or partner with another movement, make sure of the seal of the Holy Spirit regarding that ministry. Does the Holy Spirit seem to be a caged bird waiting to be loose once you put money on the table, or is the Holy Spirit already descending upon you as you hear the voice of your Heavenly Father?

Is God affirming you and confirming your calling while you are tuned in or while you are sitting in the audience, or is God held at bay until you pay? You must remember that every economy must have a driving force that moves it. In our society, our economy is driven by the stock market.

In this irreverent economy, the livestock market drives this illegal system of trading. It is the dove (Holy Spirit) that is being offered.

People are merchandising the anointing by putting a price tag on miracles, blessings, and breakthroughs. They are telling people that for a seed-gift of a certain amount of money, God can heal, deliver, and cause to prosper. The moment that they "partner" into that ministry, they have untold blessings laying in store for them. The dove is in the cage and can only be released once money is laid on the table. What a tragedy to the Body of Christ! How many people are falling for these tricks and gimmicks not seeing that the will of the Lord is for them to humble themselves, pray, and seek His face? If only people would realize that if they would turn from their wicked ways, God would forgive their sin and heal their land.

Money cannot substitute for obedience. A seed-gift cannot compensate for an unrepentant heart. If you play the livestock market, you will close the day at a loss. The Bible declares in Proverbs 14:12, as well as Proverbs 16:25, "There is a way that seems right unto a man, but the end thereof are the ways of death." How many times do people look for the way of convenience? We make poor, reckless decisions yet we expect God to cure them all with a seed-gift. We live a life of poor stewardship, unfaithful tithing, and giving sparingly, yet we expect God to reward us with a bountiful harvest, just because someone is offering livestock at a low cost!

This livestock is the dove representing the anointing that individuals are offering, while promising a quick return. Unless an individual is being led by the Spirit of God, they cannot appropriate the promises of life in the Spirit, even if they attempt to obtain them by purchase. In other words, playing the livestock market is a poor investment, and is fool's gold. When Jesus saw the selling of doves, He saw the danger in what they were doing. That's why He said that they had made the House of God a den of thieves. They were hindering the work of God, and many people were still suffering as we see later on with the blind and lame now being able to come to Him to be healed. They were thieves not only because they were attempting to profit off the anointing, but because their greed robbed the people of the opportunity for healing.

Money cannot substitute for obedience. A seed-gift cannot compensate for an unrepentant heart.

Turning the Tables

In St. Matthew 21:21 and 22, Jesus declares, "If you have faith, and doubt not, you shall not only do this which is done to the fig tree, but also if you shall say unto this mountain, be removed, and be cast into the sea, it shall be done. (22) And all things, whatever you ask in prayer, believing, you will receive." The disciples had witnessed the supernatural result of faith in action as Jesus cursed a fig tree, and it withered away immediately. They began to stare at the tree with amazement and commented on the rapid state of its withering condition.

Jesus reveals to them that faith caused this to happen, and if they believed and did not doubt, faith would cause even more miracles in their lives. This passage of scripture amongst countless others (far too many to quote) reveals this spiritual truth; faith is the currency that tenders all Kingdom transactions. If it is going to happen and it involves God, it must happen through faith. Hebrews 11:6 tells us that "Without faith it is impossible to please Him . . ." Therefore, we must understand that God only honors faith. Since faith is the currency to all of our transactions with God and His Kingdom, then it is important that this currency is available to everybody that seeks to know Him.

What would happen if you needed faith, knew where to get faith, but when you went to get it, you found that it was being sold to the highest bidder? Imagine what Jesus must have felt entering into the temple. The Bible declares in St. Matthew 21:12 that "He overthrew the tables of the moneychangers . . ." The significance of this specific act is far too profound to ignore. In three of the four gospels, the writers record that Jesus overthrew the tables of them who changed money! His contempt over what they did was so great that He physically turned over their tables.

What was the connection between the moneychangers and faith, and how does this all relate to the black market? In order for you to understand the profound significance of this, listen to what Mark's gospel declares was Jesus' words. St. Mark 11:17 declares, "And Jesus *taught,* saying unto them, Is it not written, my house shall be called of all nations the house of prayer? but ye have made it a den of thieves."

First of all, Mark records that this wasn't just a scourging or a cleansing, but also a teaching as well. What was the lesson? The lesson was that God's house was a House of Prayer for every nation, kindred, tongue, race, and people. God's house was a house that reflected His church, made up of people from every nation across the world. Not one race, culture, nation, or denomination can lay claim to Jehovah as just their God alone.

Thus, the House of God should represent physically what the church consists of spiritually. This is the message of the gospel of Jesus Christ—that God so loved the world that He gave His only Begotten Son—that whoever believes on Him shall not perish but have everlasting life. Jesus saw an act that was not only despicable, but divisive. The moneychangers were overcharging foreigners who exchanged their foreign money for the native currency, in order to make a purchase of the sacrifices. In other words, all nations couldn't benefit equally from the temple because they did not all have access to the native currency. In order to get access, they were charged exorbitant prices for the right currency.

Access to God should be granted to everyone, not just a select few. Access to this Christian faith cannot be denied to anyone because of race, color, or nationality. Our faith in God through Jesus Christ is the currency that tenders all Kingdom transactions. For the end of Hebrews 11:6 declares, "For He that cometh to God must first believe that He is, and that He is a rewarder to them who diligently seek Him." Faith begins with knowing Jesus Christ, for you must first believe that He is God.

This faith is what brings all that God has into our lives. No particular group of people has the right to hold that truth hostage from anyone. No individual class of people has the right to be moneychangers, who sit at the door of salvation, offering faith at the highest bid. The moneychangers were arrogant. The moneychangers were thieves because they were extortionists. The moneychangers were opportunists not looking to evangelize or proselytize, but to capitalize. The moneychangers were a select group of people who thought they were the only ones chosen and that everyone else looking to worship God was beneath them and had to pay a higher price. Jesus' indignation was over their discrimination! This House of Prayer was for all nations. God wanted to be Lord over all creation. God purposed through Calvary to make all nations His creation and to make disciples of every nation. This was the mystery of the cross! Not only the Jews but the Gentiles would become part of the Kingdom of God.

> **Our faith in God through Jesus Christ is the currency that tenders all Kingdom transactions.**

God had a greater plan and it included all nations. Faith should never be held captive by any particular group or class of people. God is the God of the poor, as well as the rich. God is the God of the Portuguese as well as the American. No one can set up a table at the door and charge admission to the altar of worship. Many for centuries have tried. There have been all types of propaganda in the name of religion designed to classify and qualify the have and the have-nots. But just as Jesus did in the temple thousands of years ago, so is He doing even today.

Jesus is turning the tables on every sect, race, class, group, organization, affiliation, and denomination that wishes to exclude others except it be for a high price. Jesus is turning the tables with the same righteous indignation He possessed in this text. No one will rob another group or race of people of an opportunity to know Christ as their Savior and Lord. They will be able to pray with the same faith (currency) that will produce the same results as when

God on the Black Market

Jesus cursed that fig tree, and it withered immediately. Our faith transcends our culture, as well as our crisis. God is a God who provides faith that removes mountains, regardless of the color.

Chapter 4

THE TEMPLE OF GOD

In 2 Corinthians 6:16, Paul says "And what agreement hath the temple of God with idols? For you are the temple of the living God; as God has said, "I will dwell in them, and walk in them; and I will be their God, and they shall be my people." The Bible also says in 1 Corinthians 6:19, "What? Know not that your body is the temple of the Holy Ghost which is in you, which ye have of God; and you are not your own?" Both passages of scripture reveal that we are the temple of God! As a matter of fact, listen to the words of the writer in Acts 7: 44–48. "Our fathers had the tabernacle of witness in the wilderness, as he had appointed, speaking unto Moses, that he should make it according to the fashion that he had seen. (v45) Which also our fathers that came after brought in with Jesus into the possession of the Gentiles, whom God drove out before the face of our fathers, unto the days of David; (v46) Who found favor before God, and desired to find a tabernacle for the God of Jacob. (v47) But Solomon built him a house." We saw earlier in Chapter 3 of this book how Solomon built the temple and how God received it as the place where His Name would be established. Although the tabernacle and the temple were places of God's visitation in the Old Covenant, they were not the places of God's dwelling.

In verse 48 of this same chapter in Acts, the Bible says "However, the most High dwells not in temples made with hands; as said the prophet. (v49) Heaven is my throne, and earth is my footstool: what house will you build for me? Says the Lord: or what is the place of my rest?"

In the relationship between God and man, the place of God's visitation became confused with the place of God's habitation. For in the relationship between God and man, the preferred place of God's dwelling *always* remained the same. God had always desired to dwell within the hearts of His people. Because of their rebellious ways, God could not do it. Therefore, He could only visit in an enclosed place set apart in the tabernacle and the temple, accessed only by the high priests. God's Divine Plan was not to dwell in any place made with hands, but rather that His people would receive His Spirit to dwell with them. In other words, the tabernacle and then later on the temple were just shadows of the predestined plan of God to make His abode within the hearts of every believer.

> In the relationship between God and man, the place of God's visi-

tation became confused with
the place of God's habitation.

The tabernacle in the days of Moses and the temple that King Solomon constructed symbolized God's desire for His Empowering Presence to reside in the lives of those who would follow Him. Just as surely as God had a pattern for the tabernacle under the old covenant, He has a pattern for His church under the new. The Apostle Paul recognized this sovereign plan of God when observing idolatry during one of his missionary journeys. He observed how idol worshippers were focused upon erecting temples and altars for their false gods. He endeavored to distinguish the only true and living God from all other idols by magnifying God above any supposed "god" needing a temple. Paul wanted them to know that you cannot contain God.

You cannot reduce the worship experience to a gathering within four walls of a building. The Holy One is far greater than anything that could ever be imagined. The tabernacle and the temple could only witness God's visitation. God wanted us to witness His habitation. Can you imagine how God must have felt manifesting His glory within the confines of a small place called the Holies of Holy? After all, here was the Maker and Creator of all that exists, revealing Himself behind a curtain. As awesome as the manifestation of God's presence was in the tabernacle and in the temple, it was veiled in comparison to the outpouring that God desired to take place throughout the entire world. As a matter of fact, upon

Jesus' death when the curtain of the temple was torn, not only were all of us given access to God's throne, but also to His Divine Presence.

Now God could reveal His glory before all who would believe and receive, not just the high priest. Soon all who would believe on the Lord Jesus Christ would be made a 'royal priesthood' to show forth the glory and praises of the One who brought us out of darkness into His marvelous light. That is the privilege we have today, unlike any other time in the history of our existence.

We can manifest God's Divine Purpose to reveal His glorious presence through our lives. This is why Paul calls us the temple of the Holy Spirit. God wants to set His glory upon us to the place where the world can see and know Him. That is why Paul says that our bodies are the temple of the Holy Spirit. God is a Spirit, desiring to reveal Himself in a physical and tangible way.

Like all spirits seeking a body in which to work in the earth, our Heavenly Father is looking for a physical body to fulfill His Divine Will and plan in the earth. He wants us to glorify Him in our bodies, as well as in our spirits, because they are His through the blood of Jesus Christ. Our bodies must be separated from the world and from defilement because they must reveal the holiness and righteousness of God.

The world must see God's character when they watch our lives. We become His hands and feet, and we reflect His ways as we live on this earth. There are so many believers who truly don't understand the tremendous privilege and responsibility that goes with our profession. The Spirit of God *needs* a body in which to function and through which to operate. Without this body housing the Spirit of God, God's Kingdom cannot be advanced in the earth. Without this temple of God, He cannot manifest Himself to be who He is to the world. If it is to happen in the earth, it must happen through a man. If it is to happen, it must be translated into the natural. Notice that all throughout 1 Corinthians Chapter 6, the Apostle Paul is emphasizing the importance of our own bodies. He only mentions our spirit at the end of verse 20. Our spirits are vital in containing and receiving all that is spiritual. Yet our bodies are keys in translating all that is spiritual into the natural.

God not only wants to be revered, He wants to be revealed. Our spirits revere Him; our bodies reveal Him! That is why Moses records the creation in Genesis. Revelation begins with creation! For it is the supernatural transcending into the natural in order to be realized. That is also why the Word became flesh and dwelt among us (St. John 1:14), to reveal the plan of salvation that could only be realized when Divinity entered into humanity.

Our bodies are necessary in translating and transferring all that is spiritual. Paul declares in 1 Corinthians 3:17, "If any man defile (destroy) the temple of God, him shall God destroy; for the temple of God is holy, which temple we are." What a powerful verse! Paul is presenting one of the strongest warnings in the New Testament. He calls our bodies the temple and warns against destroying this temple. God seems to be very zealous when it comes to the places in which He manifests His Presence, whether it is a church building (temple) or our bodies (temple). Anyplace where God manifests is a place where His standards are raised, where we are held accountable for how we treat it. Based upon Paul's admonition, we can now begin to superimpose the principles laid out in Chapter 3 of this book, "House of Prayer" or "Den of Thieves," and make them applicable to our own personal lives.

> God not only wants to be revered,
> He wants to be revealed.

Holy Ground

When observing Paul's admonition in 1 Corinthians 3:17, I immediately reflect upon Moses' life-changing encounter with God. For it is here in Exodus 3:5 where holiness is mentioned for the very first time. For those of us who study the Word of God, we are fully aware of the innumerable amount of times the word 'holy' is used to describe God: feasts, days, weeks, vessels of the tabernacle, and so on.

Isn't it interesting that the very first time holy is mentioned in scripture is when it is ascribed to a ground? You would think that God would first introduce man to the concept of holiness by describing Himself. It is very difficult to imagine man being able to understand the concept of holiness from a parcel of land or dirt. Yet that is exactly what God had in mind. God wanted to reveal to Moses and all creation what He had in mind for mankind, which is reiterated in 1 Corinthians 3:17. First of all, notice what happened. The angel of the Lord appeared unto Moses in a flame of fire out of the midst of a bush. Moses looked with amazement how that the bush was burning with fire, yet wasn't destroyed. It was while Moses turned to look inquisitively at the bush that God called him out of the bush.

God says something that would later on prove to be a prophetic overture of His perfect plan. In Exodus 3:5, God declares "Draw not nigh here. Put off your shoes from your feet, for the place where you stand is holy ground." Powerful! God declares that the ground on which Moses stood was holy. Why would God declare dirt as holy? What glory would come out of God manifesting His holiness through a patch of dirt? The power of God taking an otherwise useless piece of dust and transforming it into a glorious, holy ground has always been God's endeavor since He formed man from the dust of the earth, breathed into man's nostrils, and man became a living soul.

God showed Moses that the purpose for Him creating the world was that He wanted to impart His glory upon man, to reveal His holiness through man. Thus the ground in Exodus 3:15 represented man who came from the ground. Since God, who is a consuming fire, can ignite a bush and it not be consumed, He can ignite our lives and they not be destroyed.

The end result of a powerful union between a consuming fire (God), and an available bush (our lives), is a holy ground (a temple of the Holy Spirit). That is what God wanted then and still wants today.

Holy ground is a result of the supernatural overwhelming the natural. Holy ground is when the spiritual ignites the earthly. The ground wasn't holy *before* the bush burned upon it. The ground was holy *because* the bush burned upon it. The ground was holy because it held an unexplainable phenomenon, foreshadowing our salvation experience. Notice God's commandment in verse 5. God tells Moses, "Draw not nigh here . . ." Meaning, don't come any closer. It was because Moses wasn't approaching the bush to see who it was. He was approaching the bush to see why it was doing what it did. He wasn't approaching the bush to glean a closer encounter, but to get a clearer explanation. In other words, Moses' motives were wrong. God wants us to draw nigh to Him, but with the right motives and the right attitudes. That's where the defilement takes place. It takes place in the private areas of our motives. Moses, at this time, wasn't a sincere seeker, but a spectator. That would have extinguished the fire!

Next God commands that Moses "put off your shoes from your feet . . ." Why is the removal of Moses' shoes so critical to this experience? It is because the feet represent our walk, which speaks of our relationship with the Lord. When the feet are covered as they were there, they represent anything in our lives that stands between us and our Heavenly

Father, preventing His holiness from influencing us. This was a time in which Moses should have experienced firsthand the presence of God without interference.

Nothing must defile this experience, for it is out of this experience that we understand the clarion call for holiness, without which no man shall see the Lord! Nothing must dilute and contaminate this one-on-one encounter with God. This wasn't a time to have something standing in between. The shoes would have hindered Moses' experience, as so many things hinder our lives, and cause this temple not to be the holy ground that would reveal God's glory. To defile this temple is to possess something that needs to be put off. To defile this temple is to embrace an attitude or lifestyle that needs to be shed. Some things must be purged out of our lives and cast off like Moses' shoes in order for us to be the temple of the Holy Spirit. The imprint of God's Divine Plan can't be mixed with the footprints of our own way!

> **The imprint of God's Divine Plan can't be mixed with the footprints of our own way!**

A House of Prayer

Paul's admonition in 1 Corinthians 3:17, in which we are revealed to be the temple of God, causes the principles of the events that transpired in St. Matthew 21 to be superimposed in our lives. When Jesus enters into the temple and casts out all who sold and bought in the temple, the principles of His actions become templates that design the pattern for our personal walk with the Lord.

Since we are the temple of God, and the Spirit dwells in us, then the temple mentioned in this text represents our lives. This cleansing of the temple now symbolizes the salvation experience in which Christ enters into our lives and begins to first purge and purify. Notice the order of Jesus' actions. He first comes to set order in our lives by "foreclosing" on the business of the enemy. We must understand that while we were sinners, our lives were being black-marketed by the devil. The adversary's kingdom profited from our slavery.

The Bible declares in Romans 7:14 "For we know that the law is spiritual: but I am carnal, sold under sin." Paul's words seem to describe a thriving, black market that increased its profit margin as we remained enslaved to sin. He later on says, "For what I would, that do I not; but what I hate, that I do." He reveals that we were slaves to sin, incapable of rescuing ourselves from destructive patterns and despicable habits.

All the things that we knew were good to do, yet those things we didn't do. In addition, the things that we despised and had contempt for, those things we did. In other words, sin had dominion over us.

> "For the wages of sin is death . . ."
> We were getting paid, but it wasn't a paycheck. We had an income, but it wasn't an increase.

The enemy's kingdom advanced as we regressed. The devil's kingdom profited as we lost out. It was a disingenuous system of trade that had us at a deficit in which our wages would result in death. For the Bible declares in Romans 6:23 "For the wages of sin is death . . ." We were getting paid, but it wasn't a paycheck. We had an income, but it wasn't an increase. The result was a spiritual disconnection from the One who is life, which meant spiritual death, and an eternal separation from God, which is eternal death.

This was the market index under which we were operating. In the temple, this activity was occurring, and Jesus moved with righteous indignation by unseating those who perpetrated this theft. No longer was this market going to be open for business in this temple. This temple was going to be purified and freed from the control of the moneychangers.

This temple was going to be delivered from the extortionists. Jesus began to establish order in this temple by getting rid of the former authority. In St. Matthew 21:13, He declares, "It is written, my house shall be called the house of prayer, but you have made it a den of thieves."

Jesus once again reveals that the temple must be known for its prayers, just as believers must be known by their prayer lives. Since we are the temple of God, and the Spirit of God dwells in us, then our bodies must be devoted to a life of prayer and communion with God. Jesus said, "My house shall be called the house of prayer . . ." Therefore, since we are His house, we must be given to prayer in our everyday life. Prayer must be our way of life. The Bible declares in St. Luke 18:1 " And He spoke a parable unto them for this reason, that men ought to always pray, and not to faint;" In this chapter, Jesus describes in a parable a widow who persistently appeared before an unjust judge to avenge her adversary.

This woman's constant request to the judge was the reason for him granting her request. It wasn't because he regarded God, or even any man. It was because of the widow's persistence that she had her request granted.

Jesus was speaking of a continual life of prayer that would result in prayers being answered and petitions granted. Even in 1 Thessalonians 5:17, the Bible admonishes us to "pray without ceasing." Paul also declares in Ephesians 6:18, "Praying always with all prayer and supplication in the Spirit, and watching with all perseverance and supplication for all saints." The Bible is clear on how vital an active prayer life is to the success of our walk with the Lord. Our bodies that are the temple of God must become a House of Prayer.

How many excuses do we make for not having a consistent prayer life? How busy have we become that fitting prayer into our hectic schedules has become last on our "to-do" list? We obviously don't realize this, but the regime that once had control over us desires to resume its business activities. Jesus didn't overturn the moneychangers and drive out those who sold doves just so that they could come back and resume business. He intended on closing down the adversary's business once and for all, and that foreclosure would be permanent. It is constant communion with God that prevents the old man from resuscitating and becoming active again in our lives. Once Jesus purges and purifies, the only way for this black market organization, called the kingdom of Satan, to come back is if it is allowed to. We cannot give place to the devil. We cannot give him a foothold. He cannot be allowed to advertise to us a different agenda than God's agenda. His next marketing strategy won't be as obvious as blatant sinfulness.

Remember what these individuals were selling in the text. The items that were being sold were not considered instruments of sin. It is because the adversary's next scheme is to offer salvation at the price of compromise. This marketing strategy is to get you to walk with the Lord, while walking after your flesh. Then you'll abuse grace and mercy by acknowledging their importance, yet completely ignoring the importance of holiness.

Allude to God's love, not His judgments, and point to His compassion, not His contempt. Read and recognize the scriptures that point out promises, yet omit the ones that promote principles. You will then find a life that is religious not relational, forsaking a life of prayer, which is the centerpiece for all communication with God. Without a life of prayer, we will be reduced to integrating sinfulness with spirituality, which really is carnality. Carnality is spirituality purchased on the black market! It is a cheap, easy, and affordable attempt to connect with God without submitting to His authority. A life of prayer will expose the wicked ways that we have endorsed and will create an attitude of turning from them. God's universal purpose for mankind is that we be holy as He is holy. Through the holiness of the Father revealed in us, we can now be able to reconcile the lost back to Him.

So if holiness is viewed as an outdated concept reserved only for a particular denomination, then don't count on fulfilling God's destiny for your life. Notice that in 2 Corinthians 6:14–16, Paul declares "Be not unequally yoked together with unbelievers: for what fellowship has righteousness with unrighteousness? And what communion has light with darkness? (15) And what alliance has Christ with Belial? Or what part has a believer with one who says there is no God? (16) And what agreement has the temple of God with idols?" Notice how Paul's argument for separation provokes his teaching that we are the temple of the living God.

Paul understood that the next level of opposition against the church of the Lord Jesus Christ is Christians trying to merge with the world. We underestimate the powerful influence compromise has over any individual. When a person compromises, they invite Satan's influence, and the level of this influence is directly linked to the level of the compromise. That is why prayer must be the centerpiece of our existence. We must have a consistent life of devotion and communion with God. This fellowship cannot be broken or interrupted if we are going to keep out the agents that Jesus first cast out!

A House of Power

It is no coincidence that, in St. Matthew 21, once Jesus expelled the moneychangers and drove out the dove sellers from the temple *then* He began healing the blind and the lame. Deliverance begins where defilement ends! Notice the order of conversion and salvation. First, the House of God was purged and purified. Next, the House of God was to become the House of Prayer. Thirdly, the House of God became a House of Power. It is impossible to experience God's deliverance as long as the adversary's agents remain in authority.

Jesus must first expel the agents of the enemy. Satan's influence must be denounced and dethroned, *and then* Christ will set up His authority! He absolutely will not coexist with any other god. That is why Paul asks, "What agreement has the temple of God with idols?"

We must renounce our affiliation with Satan's kingdom before we can expect the Kingdom of God to be manifested in our life. This manifestation of the Kingdom of God is established through Jesus Christ and expressed by the Holy Spirit! The House of God became a House of Power, manifested through deliverance for the blind and the lame.

Just as our bodies become a House of Power, as the manifestation of the Holy Spirit becomes evident through our deliverance. The nature of sin, which produced blindness in our spiritual being, and the dominion of sin, which produced lameness in our spiritual walk, have been defeated through the power of the Holy Spirit.

The Bible declares in St. Luke 10:18 and 19 "I beheld Satan as lightening fall from heaven. (19) Behold, I give unto you power to tread on serpents and scorpions, and over all the power of the enemy: and nothing shall by any means hurt you." Jesus declares that we have been given authority over demons, and over the works of the kingdom of Satan. He emphasizes that nothing shall harm us because we have authority that exceeds the authority of the enemy. What a powerful revelation!

The enemy's power and plans over our lives *must* fail because of the authority given to us through the Holy Spirit. The Bible later declares in Acts 1:8 "But you shall receive power, after that the Holy Ghost is come upon you: and you shall be witnesses unto me both in Jerusalem, and in all Judaea, and in Samaria, and unto the uttermost part of the earth."

The promise of baptism in the Holy Spirit had been given to the disciples before Jesus' ascension, because He understood the necessity of the Holy Spirit being in full operation in the life of every believer. That is why Paul tells us in 1 Corinthians 4:16, "Know you not that you are the temple of God, and that the Spirit of God dwells in you?" Ephesians 2: 21 and 22 declares, "In whom all the building fitly framed together grows unto a holy temple in the Lord;

(22) in whom you also are built together for a habitation of God through the Spirit." We must understand that the Holy Spirit's assignment is to make us fit for God's habitation, with Jesus Christ as the chief corner stone. Jesus establishes the church, and His Spirit expresses all that the church will become. If we are to live out the gospel of Jesus Christ, it must be a life empowered by the Holy Spirit. So many people cannot understand why they haven't witnessed deliverance in their personal lives.

Deliverance begins where defilement ends

They continue to experience failures in their walk with the Lord, and find themselves spiritually powerless to the struggles of their flesh. Without the power of the Holy Spirit, one can expect a life of darkness (the blind) and dysfunction (the lame). Jesus only healed once the agents of defilement were discharged.

He would not heal while the moneychangers and sellers were still in operation. Deliverance begins where defilement ends! Notice the violent manner in which Jesus cleansed the temple. He made a scourge of cords and whipped them out of the temple, as He turned over tables and kicked over the seats of those who sold doves. This wasn't a passive display, but rather a passionate demonstration of a zeal that Christ possessed in order to establish His authority. We must realize that the kingdom of Satan is resourceful. It is a kingdom that is opportunistic and a kingdom that exploits weaknesses whenever it is given the opportunity. The moneychangers and sellers used what were ordinarily positive elements and perverted them to use for their own selfish gain. Satan's kingdom is resourceful in distorting and perverting what was once harmless and turning it into something poisonous.

This kingdom cannot be escorted out, but must be driven out! St. Matthew 11:12 declares "And from the days of John the Baptist until now the kingdom of heaven suffers violence, and the violent take it by force." This is a resourceful kingdom; therefore, it requires those that are willing to thrust and push to oppose it. That is why Jesus became so indignant and physically removed them. Furthermore, the kingdom of Satan is relentless. That is why Jesus began to immediately heal after He drove out the defilers. This was a strategic move by Jesus Christ to establish His authority within the temple to declare to every thief that this temple was now under a new command.

Notice a powerful passage of scripture that reveals the relentlessness of the kingdom of Satan. St. Luke 11:24 declares, " When the unclean spirit is gone out of a man, he walks through dry places, seeking rest; and finding none, he says, 'I will return unto my house whence I came out. And when he comes, he finds it swept and garnished. Then he goes and takes with him seven other spirits more wicked than himself; and they enter in, and dwell there: and the last state of that man is worse than the first."

What Jesus did in St. Matthew 21 reveals the order of our conversion and salvation, which establishes not only a willingness to forsake sin, but also a commitment to obedience to Christ, prayer, and being filled with the Holy Spirit.

We must be filled with the Holy Spirit, which will declare to the kingdom of Satan that our temples are occupied and controlled by a greater authority. The moment we are spirit-filled and become spirit-led, we fortify ourselves against the ensuing attacks from a relentless and resourceful adversary. Luke tells us in Chapter 11 that the unclean spirit will find no rest. It is because this spirit is displaced. It has been removed from its habitation. The unclean spirit will then inevitably return to see the state of that house. That is why our temples (bodies) must become a House of Power. Once the former authority perceives that the Spirit of God rules and resides in your life, it must concede to that spiritual reality.

A House of Perfected Praise

The moment Jesus began healing in the temple, the House of Power became a House of Perfected Praise. St. Matthew 21:15–16 declares "And when the chief priests and scribes saw the wonderful things that he did, and the children crying in the temple, and saying, 'Hosanna to the son of David', they were very displeased, (16) and said unto him, 'Do you hear what they are saying?' And Jesus said unto them 'Yeah, have you never read that out of the mouth of babes and sucklings thou hast perfected praise?'" What was now taking place fulfilled all that

God desired for His temple. Remember that God called the temple a House of Sacrifice because it was in the temple that great sacrifices were being offered. The key element of Old Testament worship was the sacrificial system.

However, since the sacrifice of Jesus Christ on the cross fulfilled this system, there was no longer any need for the shedding of blood as part of Christian worship. As a royal priesthood in the New Testament age, the church is now admonished to offer "the sacrifice of praise to God continually, that is, the fruit of our lips giving thanks to His name." (Heb.13:5) We are also called to be "a living sacrifice, holy, acceptable unto God which is your reasonable service." (Rom.12:1) The powerful truth revealed in both of these passages of scripture is that the due order of our priesthood rests in giving praises to God and living as praise to God.

As a royal priesthood, our lifestyle involves continual praise with thanksgiving, and our mission is to "show forth the praises of Him who called us out of darkness into His marvelous light." (1 Peter 2:9) The temple in St. Matthew 21 filled with the sounds of praise and thanksgiving. The temple filled with the glorious shouts of "Hosanna to the son of David." Christ was being glorified.

He was being praised for the awesome power He displayed and the authority He exhibited in driving out the defilers. According to St. Matthew 21:15, there were those who were very displeased. They were angry because the sounds of praise, thanksgiving, and the glorious shouts of "Hosanna to the son of David" were words coming from children.

Since this temple represents our bodies, then the chief priests and scribes in this text represent the spirit of religion. In this text, the religious were offended over whom they were bowing to. In our Christian walk, the spirit of religion is offended that we have to bow as children. Jesus established in the temple that only babes and those who give suck can give Him a perfected praise. It comes out of the mouth of a little child. Our praise can only be perfected when it comes from a heart that has humbled itself as a little child.

The problem with the spirit of religion is that it is haughty and high-minded. Therefore, it will always fight with the power and authority of Jesus because it refuses to submit to His Lordship. The innocence of a child is the way Jesus seeks to be worshipped. He takes great delight in the pureness of a child's heart. Most people get that confused. They mistake a child's innocence for naïvety, and they confuse being childlike with being childish. Jesus said in St. Mark 10:14, "Suffer the little children to come unto me, and forbid them not: for of such is the kingdom of God." Jesus spoke with much displeasure because His disciples tried to prevent the children from being touched by Him. As a matter of fact, the disciples even rebuked those who brought the children to Jesus. It was out of this displeasure that Jesus told them to allow the children to come to Him, and by no means should they be forbidden.

Then Jesus reveals something powerful about the Kingdom. He declares that the Kingdom of God is made up of children. Powerful!

Not only is the Kingdom of God filled with children, but the Kingdom of God is made up of children. In other words, the Kingdom is advanced through a childlike heart. Then Jesus declares in verse 15 "Verily I say unto you, whoever shall not receive the kingdom of God as a little child, he shall not enter therein." This verse has been ignored, yet it is a key to entrance into God's Kingdom or an agent that will hinder any access.

Jesus not only reveals that the Kingdom of God is made up of those with childlike trust and faith, but if anyone doesn't embrace God's Kingdom through the heart and mind of a child, they won't enter. Receiving the Kingdom of God like a child means accepting it in a humble, trustful, and willing fashion that will result in forsaking sin and acknowledging Jesus Christ as Lord and Savior. This is the only spirit that is welcomed into the Kingdom of God, because the adult mind is too religious, philosophical, skeptical, and analytical to embrace a reality that goes beyond what is seen. The children in St. Matthew 21 saw and praised God wrapped in human flesh. The children in St. Matthew 21 looked beyond the physical, and they praised Christ as the coming Messiah. That is what a perfected praise is. It is a praise that embraces the supernatural and disregards the limits of the natural. They embraced what the religious leaders rejected. They saw another realm and dimension that brought healing to the blind and lame.

> **Perfected praise is a praise that embraces the supernatural and disregards the limits of the natural.**

No doubt these were some of the children of the blind and lame, so they appreciated the Messiah's ministry and message. To them, Jesus was the King. A House of Perfected Praise is a person who will worship and praise God with childlike innocence and enthusiasm. In other words, only an individual who can completely believe God is a person who can completely praise God. Moreover, this doesn't come by adult-like reasoning, but through childlike faith in Jesus Christ.

Chapter 5

IDENTITY THEFT

The twenty-first-century thief has become more technical in his methods. As a matter of fact, the 1990s spawned a new variety of crooks called identity thieves. No longer does the profile of this type of criminal solely involve breaking and entering or robbing an individual at gunpoint. Judging from police reports and statistics, it seems that the crime of choice is identity theft. Identity theft occurs when someone uses your personal information such as your name, Social Security number, credit card number, or other identifying information without your permission to commit fraud or other crimes. Identity theft is a serious crime. People whose identities have been stolen can spend months or years and their hard-earned money cleaning up the mess thieves have made of their good name and credit record. The results are devastating. Victims may lose job opportunities, be refused loans, education, housing, cars, or even get arrested for crimes they didn't commit.[1]

In identity theft, a thief doesn't have to

encounter the possibilities of watchdogs, burglar alarm systems, or even a homeowner with a loaded firearm. Furthermore, a person who steals another individual's identity can capitalize on all the power and privileges gained by the victim. Identity theft is a crime of thought, not impulse. It is a heartless crime because it will steal and destroy any opportunity for the unsuspecting victim to achieve any type of success, and it leaves damages that are long lasting.

Oftentimes it becomes impossible to track down individuals who perpetrate this theft because by the time it is discovered, bank accounts are pilfered, credit cards are maxed out, business transactions are falsely rendered, and contract agreements are breached.[2] These kinds of crimes are not shown on any police reality shows, and they are not publicized on the evening news.

As a matter of fact, identity theft isn't entertaining because it isn't sensational. There are no weapons, exchanges of gunfire, police chases, or explosions, yet this is one of the most costly and elusive of crimes. Individuals are rarely prosecuted to the same degree of the crime because it is very difficult to equate in monetary or punitive damages the cost of the inconvenience, the feeling of being violated, or the agony of starting over. Identity theft is a cruel, vicious crime that inflicts injuries, and although they aren't life threatening, they are life altering.

Now as the Body of Christ engaging in spiritual warfare, we must not be ignorant of Satan's devices. He is our adversary who the Bible describes as a thief who comes to steal, kill, and destroy. As believers who must earnestly contend for the faith, we must understand that this thief isn't using conventional methods or traditional means. The type of theft perpetrated today by this adversary, the devil, is identity theft. He understands that his gates cannot prevail against the church, so he will attempt to cause the church to fight against itself.

Years ago, we encountered a thief who was invasive and intrusive. We witnessed the Body of Christ being attacked in untold ways as the enemy attempted to rob us of our freedoms and our rights through persecutions on all fronts. While this form of attack is still underway, the next strategy of Satan has been unleashed. He endeavors to rob the Body of Christ of its identity. This identity theft perpetrated by Satan is done by infiltrating the church through compromise and convenience, promoting a watered-down version of the gospel of Christ, and causing the Body of Christ to be ignorant of who it has been called to be. Then he misrepresents the voice of God by standing on behalf of the church, yet rejecting any teaching that upholds the doctrines of the apostles. In addition, this operation will present new doctrines and philosophies that are user-friendly and satisfy the "itching ears" by scratching them with relativism.

Make no mistake about it, this next level of spiritual warfare involves a strategizing thief who isn't acting impulsively, and the church must not be lulled asleep. Those of you reading this book may wonder how the enemy can pull this off, seeing as how identity theft requires someone to gain personal and sensitive information and pretend to be that individual in order to obtain untold advantages and privileges? First of all, an identity thief's stock in trade is your everyday transaction. Each transaction requires you to share personal information: bank and credit card account numbers, income, Social Security number, name, address, and phone numbers. An identity thief co-opts some piece of your personal information and appropriates it without your knowledge to commit fraud or theft. [3]

When we translate this into the spiritual realm, we must understand that our transactions in the kingdom are done through faith, and they span from praying and worshipping, to ministry and other spiritual matters. Any exchange between you and your Heavenly Father can be known as a transaction. Since our adversary isn't omniscient (all knowing), there are things that *must* happen in the spirit realm that precede his attack. He must gain access to information that is released during this transaction.

That is the irony about our faith and our fight. We must fight the good fight of faith, with the faith being the cause of why we are fighting to begin with. You see, we must believe in our hearts AND confess with our mouths. Faith requires that we speak what we believe (2 Cor. 4:13). Yet the moment we release it, we are also releasing personal information. Because the devil isn't all knowing, he cannot attack you with what he doesn't know about you. If he is to apply it on you, it must first apply to you! When you pray and speak things openly, the enemy can hear and attack before the answer can be manifested in your life. So there are things that he must observe and spy out. In the military, this is called Intelligence. In identity theft, it is called transaction.

If he is to apply it on you, it must first apply to you!

When we understand that the members within the Body of Christ cannot afford to be ignorant of who they are or of Satan's schemes, we will seek to understand the One who " . . . called us to glory and virtue, whereby we are given great and precious promises: that by these we might be partakers of the divine nature, having escaped the corruption that is in the world through lust." (2 Peter 1:3–4) Growing in the knowledge of Jesus Christ will protect us against identity theft by enlightening us on who we are in Him and what we have been called to do for Him.

THE TEMPTATION IN THE WILDERNESS

In St. Matthew, Chapter 4, a powerful series of events unfolds. This is one of the greatest passages of scripture because what transpires here has the potential of nullifying the prophecies of the Old Covenant and disqualifying the premise of the New Covenant. St. Matthew 4: 1–11 are such key scriptures that their significances possibly may never be fully understood or appreciated, but in light of the truths laid out in this book, I must draw upon them. First of all, let's understand that the New Covenant is based upon the death, burial, and resurrection of Jesus Christ, as well as His ascension. However, it is His ministry that bolstered Him to the cross. The legitimacy of His ministry on earth validated the purity and potency of His bloodshed upon the cross! Meaning, how Jesus lived on earth and the type of ministry He led directly influenced the significance of Calvary. If Jesus lived any kind of way, established a ministry that operated under any kind of standard and influence, then even if He went to the cross under the same conditions described in all four gospels, His suffering would have all been for nothing.

    He had to be a perfect, sinless Lamb without blemish or spot. This sinless life meant He could be at all points tempted, yet He must remain without sin. (Heb. 4:15) He had to have become sin for us, yet not ever knowing sin. (2 Cor. 5:21) This sin would have been not only that of commission, but of omission. Therefore, not only was Jesus tempted to do every despicable and deplorable act known to man, but He also was tempted to NOT do every divine and pre-destined act revealed by God. That is what makes St. Matthew 4 so critical, because it would indelibly affect His entire ministry. It was a strategic attack by the enemy right before Jesus' public ministry was about to begin. The tempter came to Him in St. Matthew 4:3 as a thief. Not as an invasive and intrusive robber, but an identify thief trying to steal the identity of the church through the Head of the Church. Then instead of trying to stop Jesus from ministering, this thief would try to influence the type of ministry that Jesus would have.

Once Satan can influence a ministry, he has just stolen that ministry's identity! Let's see how he attempted to do this. The Bible declares that the tempter came to Him and said, "If you are the Son of God, command these stones be made bread." Since identity theft requires that the victim's personal information be released through transactions, there was some personal information released earlier regarding His Son-ship. Earlier in St. Matthew 3, a transaction between the Father and His Son had taken place.

> Once Satan can influence a ministry, he has just stolen that ministry's identity!

Jesus walked in obedience and was baptized of John, because He said "For this is happening to fulfill all righteousness." In verse 16, the Bible declares that Jesus "After he was baptized, went up immediately out of the water: and the heavens were opened unto Him, and He saw the Spirit of God descending like a dove, and lighting upon Him." Then verse 17 declares a powerful transaction between the Father and the Son. This was very personal because it expressed God's thoughts concerning His Son's act of obedience. This statement reveals the personality of the Father in a way unlike any other time in history.

The writer, Matthew, records words from not just a Creator, but from a Father. These words were intimate, personal, and revealing. God in verse 17 was sharing His heart. In God's heart was immense pleasure and sheer joy over His Son's decisions, which culminated in baptism. This baptism must have expressed sincere devotion and complete submission to God's Divine Plan. Jesus, in this act of obedience, sealed His dedication to fulfilling the will of His Father in the earth. Thus God's voice spoke audibly and no doubt, very publicly. "This is my beloved Son, in whom I am well pleased." What a powerful exchange from earth to heaven, and then from heaven to earth.

However, in the next verse of the ensuing chapter, Jesus is led by the Spirit into the wilderness to be tempted of the devil. If the devil is to apply it on you, it must first apply to you. What the devil must have overheard during that personal yet public exchange at the Jordan was that God had just confirmed His Son. What the devil must have concluded was that Jesus was following in the path laid out by His Eternal Father. Therefore, this thief's response was to present temptations that would cause the Son to deviate from His Father's plan.

If the enemy could get Jesus to doubt His identity, then this would cause His ministry to spiral into a campaign of proving Himself. This would have altered His focus, resulting in compromises so severe that they would devastate His relationship with the Father and disrupt the plan of God for the world. That is why the tempter said, "If thou be the Son of God . . ." This was an attempt to rob Jesus of His identity. It was more about what the devil was trying to get Jesus to doubt than what he was trying to get Jesus to do.

The first temptation was for Jesus to command that stones be made bread. The devil wasn't hungry, but he knew that Jesus was. The first temptation was to lure Jesus into a ministry of self-gratification, moving independent of God. What is required to thwart this attack is a disciplined spirit. God wants us to have discipline, in which we can bring our flesh under subjection.

We must be able to discipline our lives so that they aren't led by emotions or impulses. In order for that to happen, we must be resolved to remain completely obedient to our Heavenly Father. That is why Jesus' first response to the devil was that "man shall not live by bread alone, but by every word proceeding out of the mouth of God." Jesus was establishing to the devil that His dependency was totally upon His Father. He would not act independent of God, even if it meant He must deny Himself of what His body craved. God's plan MUST have preeminence. This is where our identity rests. Every church opened in the name of Jesus Christ, and every believer professing to be a follower of Jesus, cannot seek to satisfy themselves and then qualify their decisions as if God wanted them to do it. We cannot go through life seeking to use our God-given authority for self-gain.

Jesus had the power to command anything to become whatever He wanted it to become, and it had to become it. Commanding stones to be made bread didn't require a great leap of faith, but it did require a giant step out of God's plan. Jesus even said, "The Son can do nothing of himself, but what he sees the Father do: for what things he does, these also do the Son likewise." (St. John 5:19) Dependency was upon God completely! He later on declares, "Believe that I am in the Father, and the Father in me? The words that I speak unto you, I speak not of myself: but the Father that dwells in me, he does the works." (St. John 14:10)

Jesus' response to the enemy was based upon a relationship He had with His Father that superseded all other requests or demands. If God did not command it, then He wouldn't either. Our power and authority must always operate under God's authority, otherwise it is abuse and misuse of power. That is the type of ministry the devil wanted Jesus to have, and that is the type of ministry the devil wants the church to possess. He wants a body of believers who will act independent of God, appropriating the principles of faith wherever they choose to, and expect God to respond. We must live by every word that God has spoken, not editing them to fit our lifestyles.

We must come up to the standards of God's will, not try and bring Him down to our standards. Remember, bread alone won't satisfy the hunger of the inner man. Using faith to get what we want will not get us what we really need. What will bring fulfillment to our spirit is what God requires. This fulfillment won't come from a stone or anything else that is in the earth. It will only come from your Heavenly Father, when you submit yourself to His will.

God on the Black Market

FRAUD

The next temptation in the wilderness reveals the strategy of this identity thief. He endeavors to fraudulently appropriate scriptures to use for his own selfish gain. This is like an identity thief opening a new account and using the name of the unsuspecting victim in order to access the privileges of their positive credit history. This is called fraud. This is a misrepresentation of another person's identity. In the wilderness, the devil took Jesus into the Holy City and set Him on the pinnacle of the temple. After this strategic positioning, he then tells Jesus, "If you are the Son of God, cast yourself down . . ." The first interesting thing is the fact that this solicitation by the adversary to Jesus was made after he positions Him on the top of the temple.

There are two types of emotions that an individual experiences when placed in such a lofty position: They will experience feelings of vulnerability or invincibility. Either this position will produce fear and panic from such dizzying heights, or it will produce arrogance and pride from sitting in the highest position. Since the devil's kingdom is advanced through fear, one possibility is that the devil's motive for taking Jesus to such heights was to provoke a spirit of fear. Yet the devil's kingdom is also advanced through pride, because it was pride that caused his fall. Therefore, it is quite possible that he wanted Jesus to adopt a spirit of pride that would influence His ministry.

I submit to every reader that his goal was to produce an attitude of invincibility, not vulnerability. In other words, his desire was to get Jesus to adopt a spirit of pride that would control His actions. The next verse confirms my position. For the devil tells Jesus in St. Matthew 4:6, "If you are the Son of God, cast yourself down: for it is written, He shall give his angels charge concerning thee: and in their hands they shall bear thee up, lest at any time you dash your foot against a stone." Instilling fear couldn't have been the motive of the enemy, because jumping from a high pinnacle would require Jesus to possess thoughts of invincibility.

These words from the adversary were laced with an arrogance that suggested Jesus could do whatever He wanted to do, and because He is the Son of God, the heavenly hosts were obligated to come to His defense. Jesus could do something so purposefully reckless just because He is the Christ, and God had to support Him. What an arrogant proposal given by the devil! He misrepresented Psalms 91, fraudulently using Holy Scripture in order to achieve his evil intentions. His intentions were to use God's own words in order to influence the ministry of Jesus, who is the Word made flesh. He perverted the scriptures and slanted them to fit his agenda. He was trying to convince Jesus that His Son-ship gave Him privileges that repealed God's standards. He proposed that Jesus take advantage of God's mercy and pleasure, throwing Himself down casually and carelessly and watching God rescue Him by sending His angels to "bare him up."

Leadership isn't a license for loose behavior. Just because we can do it, doesn't mean we should. Our standing in a lofty position doesn't give us licensed permission. That is why Jesus told the devil, "Thou shall not tempt the Lord thy God." In this one verse, verse 7, Jesus disqualifies any purposeful behavior that seeks to test God's faithfulness. We are not to tempt God. Our discipleship involves complete obedience to the Lordship of Jesus Christ. The moment Jesus would have agreed with the adversary and threw Himself down from the pinnacle of the temple, He would have violated the conditions of God's protection.

There are conditions that *must* be met if God is going to release heaven to come to our aide. St. Matthew 4:7 finds Jesus discouraging willful disobedience that attempts to force God to take action. Jesus understood that His Father affirmed Him earlier when He ascended from the water. His Father told Him how pleased He was. Now the adversary was attempting to coerce Jesus into taking advantage of this relationship. How often does this occur in our own lives? We are tempted to do something that we know is outside of God's will for our lives, but we misappropriate scripture in order to validate our decisions. This is so easy to do.

Leadership isn't a license for loose behavior.

Michael Lowery

It really isn't difficult to trespass against God. It is even easier to use scriptures to support it. The truth be told, this scripture wasn't even completed, because in Psalms 91 God reveals that our dwelling in His secret place will protect us. We don't have to fear any terror by night, nor arrows that fly by day. The Bible promises us that a thousand shall fall at our side and ten thousand at our right hand, but none of this shall come close to us. Later on God promises that no evil shall befall us nor any plague shall come to the place of our dwelling.

The thief in St. Matthew 4 attempted to rob the Body of Christ of this truth and painted a different picture using the broad strokes of his misinterpretation. He took two verses that were nestled in the confines of a context of scripture that revealed our protection, and he omitted the revelation of his own future. For in the verse following his misquote, we are promised authority to tread upon the lion and adder. We are then told that the young lion and the dragon shall we trample under foot. The devil conveniently left out the truth regarding his fate. He committed fraud, and this same tactic is being used to rob the Body of Christ of its identity.

We are told lies from the enemy disguised as truths based upon scripture, but they are perverted truths which omit the consequences of our recklessness. They are distorted in order to convince people that they are justified in their actions. This is a black-marketing scheme of the adversary to commit fraud in getting us to believe a lie. This lie is the truth misinterpreted.

There are lies that are blatant, which are easily recognizable. Then there are lies that are truths that have been perverted. In the end, it's all a lie. If anyone believes these lies and abandons his position with God, as the enemy proposed to Jesus, this willful act of disobedience will result in no angelic host waiting to assist him. Death and destruction will be waiting to embrace him.

POWER STARVATION

The Bible declares in St. Matthew 4:2 that Jesus was hungry afterward. Now we expect Him to be hungry; after all, He did fast forty days and forty nights. We are not surprised that the devil approaches Him with an initial temptation that offered Christ being satisfied with food. When the Bible declares that Jesus was hungry, perhaps we only begin to view His hunger from a natural perspective because we only associate this hunger with food. Maybe our presumption has caused us for years to miss a powerful revelatory truth that could assist us in our walk with the Lord.

There is something that the enemy proposes in verses 8 and 9 that extend beyond the borders of this premise, far beyond a meal. As a matter of fact, verses 8 and 9 are so directly connected to verse 2 that they broaden the scope of the "hunger" that is mentioned here. In verse 8 and 9, the Bible tells us that the devil took Jesus up into a very high mountain and showed Him all the kingdoms of the world and the glory of them. He then offers all of them to Jesus for worship.

Earlier in this book, I examined this verse and saw materialism as a main catalyst to the kingdom of Satan's expansion. This section reveals another dynamic to the kingdom of Satan's expansion. Not only is materialism a driving force behind the black-marketing strategy of our adversary, but he also uses power as a lure.

One of the greatest weapons of the enemy is our starvation for power. Every since the fall of man in the Garden of Eden, each generation has witnessed atrocities on a grand scale because of leaders' unquenchable thirst for power. Whether it involves tyranny and dictatorship in Third-World countries or governments within industrialized societies, what lies at the heart of every political and social fallout is someone wanting more authority.

Since the beginning of time, man has sought ways to be equal with God. This perverted way of thinking that was found in Lucifer is manifested through power struggles throughout the course of history. When reading world history, I always recalled kings and rulers never having enough territory; they felt it necessary to invade other countries. Once again, remember the serpent's temptation to Adam and Eve in the garden. He said, "You shall be as gods, knowing good and evil." Once man took from the fruit of the tree of knowledge of good and evil, it took mankind on an insatiable course for more power. No power is ever enough.

In St. Matthew, Chapter 4, the devil took Jesus on a very high mountain. He endeavored to make Jesus feel comfortable at being on top. This was a strategic attempt to provoke a mindset of independence and autonomy. Next, the enemy showed Him all the kingdoms of the world and the glory of them. The devil tempted Jesus with power. The hunger in verse 2 wasn't merely about a strong desire for food, but verses 8 and 9 reveal the enemy's hope of this being a hunger for power. The devil wanted Jesus to be starving for power. In verse 2, he found out that Jesus wasn't starving for provision. In verse 6, he discovered that Jesus wasn't starving for protection. Soon in verse 10, he will discover that Jesus wasn't starving for power. Power starvation is a tool the enemy uses to rob the Body of Christ of its identity.

> Once man took from the fruit of the tree of knowledge of good and evil, it took mankind on an insatiable course for more power.

People are willing to do whatever it takes to achieve a certain status in the church and in the world, whether it is a position or a title, and will harm anyone standing in the way. They will wreck relationships and ruin ministries. Eventually, this attitude will make the Body of Christ impotent. So in seeking for more power, the church will lose the power it has already been given. In St. Mark, Chapter 9, the Bible records a time in which all of the disciples were approached by a man who brought to them his son who had a dumb spirit.

This spirit dashed the boy violently as he foamed at the mouth, gnashed with his teeth, and pined away. Yet the Bible says that this man had to bring his demoniac boy to Jesus because the disciples couldn't cast out this spirit. They were impotent. Yet earlier in St. Mark 6: 7–13, Jesus had given them power (authority) over unclean spirits, and they cast out many devils and anointed many with oil who were sick and healed them.

Something happened between Chapter 6 and Chapter 9. How could they go from casting out devils and healing the sick at one point, to being impotent and unable to cast out a spirit at another? Something revealing happens in St. Mark 9. The disciples asked Jesus why they could not cast this spirit out. No doubt they were perplexed after having been able to do that and more beforetime. St. Mark 9:29 declares, "And he said unto them, 'This kind can come forth by nothing, but by prayer and fasting.' "

There has been much debate and speculation about what Jesus meant by "this kind." Was He talking about a certain type of spirit? Was this boy's demonic possession greater than the others? Was this dumb spirit more powerful than the prior ones? Did it take more praying for this one than those at prior times? What caused their impotence? It wasn't until shortly thereafter that we are given a probable cause to their impotence. Jesus arrives in a house after reaching Capernaum, and He asks them, "What was it that you disputed among yourselves a while ago?"

Apparently, there was brewing among them a great dispute over who would be the greatest. They were arguing over who would sit where in His kingdom. They were fighting over power. This dispute was private, but revealed through public failure. Lying at the root of their dispute was a cancer that spread throughout their ministry to the degree that it produced impotence. No doubt they had begun to enjoy the authority and position they were already given, but somewhere in their ministry, it wasn't enough. They wanted a higher position. This starvation for more power brought a real dispute between them.

Can you imagine grown men fighting over a position? It happens in churches across America. Ministries are torn apart because of a cancerous spirit that can never be content with the authority it has already been given. What a tragedy to the Body of Christ! It was because of this, I believe, they found themselves unable to do what they once could do. Pride had set in, and it stirred up a thirst for more power. That is why Jesus revealed to them that this kind could only come out through prayer and fasting. The prayer and fasting purposed to bring humility to the individuals demonstrating authority. The prayer was to stay connected to the source of our authority, and the fasting was to keep out the spirit of pride.

A life of prayer shows complete reliance upon God, not on one's self. Jesus taught them that if they wanted to be first, they must become last of everybody and servant to everyone. He revealed that this posture of servitude keeps one from starving for power, because it focuses on other people's needs. That is why the enemy could not influence Jesus to worship him, and in exchange, he would give Jesus power. It is because Jesus did not come to be over the kingdoms of the world. He did not come for the glory of the world's power. He came not to be served, but to serve.

That is why He connected servant-hood to worship. His answer to the devil was "You shall worship the Lord thy God, and Him only shall you serve." The worship of God involves serving Him. This service to Him is done by taking on the form of a servant. The mind of Christ wasn't interested in power, position, and prestige. Christ was only interested in serving His Father by serving mankind. That is why the Bible declares, "But he made himself of no reputation, and took upon him the form of a servant, and was made in the likeness of men: And being found in fashion as a man, he humbled himself, and became obedient unto death, even the death of the cross." (Phil.2:7–8)

Jesus wasn't lured by power. Jesus wasn't weakened by being upon a very high mountain either, because He already took on the form and attitude of a servant. So instead of exalting Himself like the adversary wanted Him to do, God highly exalted Him, "and gave him a name that is above every name: That at the name of Jesus every knee should bow, of things in heaven, and things in earth, and things under the earth; And that every tongue should confess that Jesus Christ is Lord, to the glory of God the Father." (Phil.2:10–11) Once we humble ourselves and take on the attitude of a servant, we will no longer be power starved. In fact, we will find fulfillment in serving others, even in places of obscurity.

Chapter 6

IDENTITY CRISIS

The temptation in the wilderness was over. Jesus had conquered the devil and thwarted his attacks with the written Word of God. This identity thief could not get the Son of God to doubt His identity, nor could he gain access to the church in order to steal her identity. All attempts in the wilderness failed. Yet St. Luke 4:13 declares that when the devil had ended all the temptations, he departed from Him for a season. The words "for a season" revealed that this relentless enemy would at some point return to try again. Thus another attack was imminent. Now we don't read anywhere in the gospels where this kind of attack from the enemy recurs, but we are fully aware that his desired results are visible within the Body of Christ today. We are not certain at what point the enemy returned to tempt Christ again while He was on earth, but we are certain that he did return after Christ ascended because the Body of Christ seems to be exhibiting signs that it has allowed these enticements to ensnare her. You see, there are two avenues through which this identity thief could enter and gain access to the Body of Christ: through the Head of the Body or through the members of the Body. In the wilderness, he tried to gain access through the Bridegroom (St. Matt. 9:15; 25:1). Now he endeavors to gain control through the Bride (Rev.21:2, 9).

The Bride of Christ, which is the church, much like Eve in the Garden of Eden, has allowed Satan to gain access into God's sovereign plan. The devil's strategy in both instances is to deceive the "weaker vessel" (1Pet.3:7) into believing a lie by using her ignorance of her own identity against her, enticing her with an opportunity for more power, and luring her out of her ordained position. This disorder would leave her uncovered and vulnerable to satanic influence. The Bible clearly says in 1 Timothy 2:14 that Adam was not deceived, but the woman being deceived was in the transgression. The Last Adam wasn't deceived either, but the church represented as the woman has fallen under deception and is now walking in transgression. Now we see professed believers seeking bread from stones, casting themselves down from dangerous places, and worshipping the devil, just like the adversary tried to get Jesus to do in the wilderness.

Look at these temptations again! Seeking bread from a stone is living independent of God's authority and satisfying one's cravings and impulses. Isn't that typical of the society in which we live? Every lifestyle is acceptable along with its impulses and cravings. The churches are even modifying their bylaws and altering their doctrines in order to accommodate these lifestyles. Leaders are simply afraid of a fallout, so they refuse to draw a line in the sand as to what is acceptable and unacceptable Christian behavior.

The Body of Christ refuses to judge matters because of the fear of her being told that she is judging. Secondly, believers are casting themselves down from dangerous places, meaning sinning willfully, citing the fact that we are under grace and not under the law. There is a strong influence of "tolerance" that has perverted the scriptures to mean that God will tolerate willful disobedience. The new "doctrines" being touted in many churches preach mercy and grace, not judgment. Rather than embracing the spiritual truths of our being the sons of God, these new philosophies continue to refer to us as mere sinners.

Therefore, the inherent attitude associated with this ideology is that we are powerless to the impulses and influences of sin, and we can expect heaven to "bare us up" as we get back up again. Finally, we are bowing to the devil because of our willingness to do whatever it takes for more power and glory. On the surface, this quest for more power doesn't seem like satanic worship, but it is. This requires believers to seek power and glory through worldly acceptance, desiring to be perceived positively in the eyes of the secular world.

Michael Lowery

The only begotten Son of God knew who He was. Now if only the "sons of God" knew who they were.

Our obsession over material things and our quest for secular acceptance and influence have caused these things to be our gods. To make these things the object of our pursuits is to make these things the objects of our worship! At the head of these things is Satan himself, who planted them deceitfully in our view as he did Jesus in the wilderness. Therefore, in seeking the glory of these things, we are worshipping the devil. Somehow, the devil accomplished his mission in the wilderness, only he didn't succeed with Christ. The only begotten Son of God knew who He was. Now if only the "sons of God" knew who they were.

Jesus did not have an identity crisis because He knew Whom He served. Therefore, the devil tempting Him by using the words "If thou be the Son of God..." proved ineffective. However, the believer today cannot look the adversary in the face and confidently withstand against him if they are ignorant to who they are. Furthermore, Christians cannot continue to walk in compromise and expect to be effective in their Christian walk. Son-ship requires boldness that will stand upon the Word of God regardless of the persecutions. Otherwise, this identity crisis will be inherited by the next generation who will completely redefine Christianity altogether!

"Who Are We To Judge?"

The radio blared on this particular Sunday morning, as people called in to respond to a question posed by the radio personality. His question to the listening audience was whether he should play a Christian song released by a secular artist. I immediately turned up the volume as my interest was peaked over hearing the opinions of the respondents. I was surprised at the overwhelming feelings of people who agreed that this song should be added into the regular rotation, and how vehemently opposed they were to any other opinion regarding the racy, raunchy lyrics of this artists' secular material.

One woman said of the artist, "He is talented, and he is making a song about Jesus Christ. And furthermore, who are we to judge?" The radio personality's response was that he wasn't judging but rather just expressing his opinion. He was adamant about not being confused as a judge. His voice rose quickly to retract any words he may have used which could have been misinterpreted as judging. The end result found the song from this artist being added to the Gospel music's regular rotation list.

Judging is not only a right of every born-again believer, it is our Christian responsibility!

I could not stop thinking about this question posed by that caller. Maybe because it was really a rhetorical question based upon a position that believers had no right to judge. Maybe because it was a statement disguised as a question that criticized anyone for taking a stand. This question was really a viewpoint posing as a question that denigrated anyone who dare assume the role as judge over spiritual matters. How many times have you heard it or have even said with your own words, "Who are we to judge?" The world has repeated this over and over again, and Christians have assimilated to this way of thinking. We have been told by secular influences that it isn't right to judge, and we have been persecuted and reviled for our biblical position on social issues.

Because we want to be viewed by the world as a group of people with arms opened wide to receive every lifestyle, we shy away from any position that would be perceived as judging. Not to mention, we have misinterpreted the message of Jesus in St. Matthew 7:1 where Jesus declares, "Judge not, that you be not judged . . ." This caller on the radio had no idea that she represented the opinions of millions of people who, although professing Christianity, actually consider judging unscriptural. This is a result of believers who are ignorant to whom they are in Christ.

Judging is not only a right of every born-again believer, it is our Christian responsibility! But because we refuse to judge matters, as a result, we find ourselves endorsing alternative lifestyles and erroneous ways of thinking. First of all, let us examine St. Matthew 7:1. Jesus condemns the criticism of others, while ignoring one's own faults. Verse 1 cannot stand independent of verses 3 and 4, for this is one continuing thought. Jesus was speaking to religious hypocrites who stood in judgment of individuals, while they themselves stood in violation of sin. They had a beam or plank in their own eyes, yet they were criticizing a speck of dust in the eyes of other individuals.

This was self-righteousness, and it led to erroneous judgment. That is why He warned them that the same judgment they placed on other individuals would return back upon them. This wasn't a scripture that condemned judgment from saints who walked as the righteous seed of the Father. He wasn't referring to those who were now called the "sons of God." This was to the Scribes and Pharisees who weren't qualified or even capable of standing in the honorable position as judge when they themselves were guilty. This absolutely does not apply to the Body of Christ!

We are not to sit passively and allow sin and immorality to run its course. We are given authority to bind and loose (St. Matt. 16:19), to remit and retain sins (St. John 20:23), and to release peace or judgment (St. Matt. 10:12–15). These are just a few examples of the authority given to the ones the Bible calls the "righteousness of God in Christ" (2 Cor. 5:21).

When an individual says, "Who are we to judge?" they are ignorant to the fact that the saints shall judge the world! (1 Cor. 6:2) They are also ignorant to the fact that the saints shall judge angels! (1

Cor. 6:3) They are oblivious to the fact that the saints are given an apostolic right to judge "things that pertain to this life" (1 Cor. 6:4). They are unaware of the fact that the saints *must* judge matters of the law amongst themselves, not taking these matters to the unjust courts (1 Cor. 6:1–8). The truth of the matter is, we are supposed to judge. That is why this question is posed in ignorance. The Bible even declares "For if we would judge ourselves, we should not be judged." (1 Cor. 11:31) The issue isn't if we can judge. The issue is that we don't judge! Just think about this. St. Matthew 4: 3 declares that the devil came to Jesus and said if He was the Son of God, command that stones be made bread.

    We know by reading this text that it was the devil, but what if this tempter didn't look like or even sound like the devil? What if to Jesus this tempter came embodied as someone He both knew and trusted? *What if the tempter came disguised?* Or, what if this tempter did not approach Jesus in human form, but was disguised as a thought or an idea? What if this was an internal struggle in which the devil tried to influence the mind of Jesus, by presenting thoughts which seemed like they came from God, but were contrary to the will of the Father?

    We naturally superimpose our imagination over this wilderness experience and place an image of Satan in front of Jesus, but that isn't fair considering that we wrestle not against flesh and blood, and that our fight is in the realm of the spirit, and in the region of the mind. Therefore, it isn't safe to assume what the tempter looked or sounded like.

It is more important that we understand what the Bible declares in 1 John 4:1. "Beloved, believe not every spirit, but try the spirits whether they are of God: because many false prophets are gone out into the world." This verse means that we must test and judge every spirit claiming to be speaking for God. If it isn't right for us to judge, then Jesus would have began commanding stones to be made bread.

He would have moved independent of God and started a ministry seeking self-gratification and fulfillment, satisfying each and every impulse. Instead, Jesus *judged* this spirit and found it not to be an encouraging word from an ally of God, but rather a temptation from the adversary to lure Him away from total obedience to the will of His Father.

That is why we *must* judge in order to keep from being snared by the enemy. We *must* judge thoughts, ideas, words, and especially deeds. We certainly are not given the authority to prejudge. That is called prejudice, and the only results from that are condemnation and discrimination. We are not given permission by our Heavenly Father to adopt a self-righteous and judgmental spirit that condemns a soul to hell. However, judging is both our right and responsibility if we are walking upright before God.

The judgments of a believer are based upon discerning matters of righteousness and unrighteousness. Contrary to the judgment of the Scribes and Pharisees handed down in the courtroom of hypocrisy, the righteous judgements of the believer are the result of the verdicts read by the jury of grace and mercy, with love serving as the foreman. If we can stand in a courtroom and respect a man or woman as having the power to decide our fate just because they have credentials and sit on a bench, how much more can we stand in position to decide matters of right and wrong when we have been created in Christ!

Saint or Sinner Saved by Grace?

The enemy has successfully lured us into an identity crisis, which finds us calling ourselves everything except what the Bible says we are! In an effort to not appear "holier than thou," we have refused to call ourselves what God calls us. Rather, we have renamed ourselves "sinners" who are saved by grace. The problem with that statement is that it is simply not true! Nowhere in Holy Scripture is a child of God called a sinner. As a matter of fact, even the scripture that reveals that we are saved by grace doesn't even refer to us as sinners. It declares, "By grace are you saved through faith, and not of yourselves. It is the gift of God, and not of works, lest any man should boast." (Eph.2:8–9) This chapter reveals that not only are we no longer sinners, but that we were quickened together with Christ, and we are raised up together and made to sit together in heavenly places in Christ Jesus.

This establishes our position in Christ that isn't at all connected to a life that passed as old things are passed away, but this connection is to all things becoming new as we were raised with Christ. This is a far cry from being called a sinner. This type of thinking has misled people and created an atmosphere of weakness and vulnerability to the control and condemnation of sin. The identity crisis suffered by many believers is the result of this ignorance of what God calls us in scripture. (For scriptures that declare a few of the names our Heavenly Father calls us, please see the list below.) Nowhere in scripture are we called sinners after our conversion! As a matter of fact, the Bible declares "knowing this, that our old man is crucified with him, that the body of sin might be destroyed, that from now on we should not serve sin . . . Likewise reckon yourselves to be dead indeed unto sin, but alive unto God through Jesus Christ our Lord." (Rom.6:6 and 11)

The more we call ourselves sinners, the more we invite an atmosphere and attitude of sin to permeate our lives. However, the moment we agree with God concerning who He calls us to become, we will continue to transform into that new creation. That is what Jesus did in St. Matthew 3, even before the tempter proposed that He cast himself down from the pinnacle of the temple. Jesus had embraced His Sonship before ever going into the wilderness; therefore, any attempts at questioning His position with God were futile. He agreed with His Father on Whom He called Him to be.

Our minds must be renewed to everything God establishes in His Word, especially our position with Him. This is how the enemy steals our identity. He deceives us into believing that calling ourselves sinners is a way of showing humility, just as Jesus throwing Himself down would show His humble dependency upon God, but just the opposite of that is true! It is actually stubborn pride. When God calls us one thing, but we call ourselves something else, it becomes stubbornness and pride. It is a blatant refusal to agree with an eternal God on what He has established, but rather to exalt one's own opinion above God's Word! The result of this stubborn pride is idolatry. That is why Samuel told Saul in 1 Sam. 15:23, "For rebellion is as the sin of witchcraft, and stubbornness is as iniquity and idolatry . . ." There are many books written about rebellion and witchcraft, but not many about stubbornness.

Stubbornness is just as dangerous as witchcraft!! It makes a god out of one's own opinion and idea! No one sees this as pride, but it is the most dangerous form of pride because it covertly disguises itself as humility, all the while denying the power of God who declares a thing from the beginning. It also denies the power of the cross, because it refuses to accept what we now have become in Christ. It points to our sinfulness, not Christ's righteousness. If we are sinners, then Christ did not rise from the dead. If we are sinners, then we cannot be saved by grace. Do you see how insidious this statement is?

You cannot be a sinner and saved by grace at the same time, because the moment this grace is activated, faith is released. This faith positions us in

Christ, in whom there is no sin. Therefore, we cannot be a sinner if we are created in Christ, for in Christ there is no sin at all (1Pet.2:22). Until we declare first to ourselves and then to the world what God has called us to be, we will continue to live a life of weakness and vulnerability. We must agree with God concerning our identity and reject any inferences to an old life that simply no longer exists.

What God calls us in Holy Scripture:

- Saints (1 Cor. 1:2)
- Sons of God (Rom. 8:14)
- God's elect (Rom. 8:33)
- His workmanship (Eph.2:10)
- Holy and beloved (Col. 3:12)
- Believers (1Tim. 4:12)
- Ambassadors (2 Cor. 5:20)
- General assembly of the firstborn (Heb. 12:23)
- Disciples (St. John 8:31)
- Members of the Body of Christ (1 Cor. 12:27)
- The righteousness of God in Christ (2 Cor. 5:21)

> The more we call ourselves sinners, the more we invite an atmosphere and attitude of sin to permeate our lives. However, the moment we agree with God concerning who He calls us to become, we will continue to transform into that new creation.

BRIBERY

You must understand how relentless and resourceful this enemy is. He endeavors to ensnare God's people at any cost, and he will even "sweeten the deal" in order to accomplish his goal. In St. Matthew 4:8, the tempter showed Jesus all the kingdoms of the world, along with the glory of them. The next verse finds the tempter offering Jesus all "these things," yet the Bible clearly establishes that "The earth is the Lord's, and the fullness thereof; the world and they that dwell therein." (Psalms 24:1).

How could the devil offer Jesus things that clearly belonged to Jesus? We all are aware that God created the heavens and the earth, so what right had the tempter to offer Jesus things that had been God's from the beginning?

It is interesting that the Bible declares that the tempter showed Jesus "all the kingdoms of the world." The kingdoms of the world are based upon worldly methods of compromise, earthly power, political maneuvering, violence, and popularity. [5] These all comprise the black market, and they work together to manipulate and control many lives for Satan's evil schemes. This was not how Jesus operated, but yet the devil showed Jesus all of this. He attempted to bribe Jesus with these things because of the hunger that Jesus experienced while walking in the wilderness.

People with kingdoms and glory are never hungry. Individuals who have popularity and earthly power never go without luxuries, much less necessities. That is why the tempter could offer Jesus these things, because these weren't the things that Jesus possessed or even wanted to own.

His Kingdom is not of this world (St. John 18:36). The Kingdom that Jesus spoke of was invisible and rested in the hearts of those submitted to the rule of the Heavenly Father. The glory of the kingdoms of the world contradicted everything Jesus stood for, because they were built upon materialism and earthly power. Therefore, the devil could offer this to Jesus because this is what he possessed. He never once told Jesus to stop ministering. He tried to influence Jesus' ministry by means of bribery.

Jesus would never have to worry about hunger or lack. There would be no need to stay at different homes or to feed thousands with just two fish and five loaves of bread. As a matter of fact, any miracle that spurned out of need or lack wouldn't be necessary because His ministry would have a corporate sponsor. Jesus could rest easier because He would have ships to carry Him across seas instead of fishermen's boats, horses with chariots to ride upon instead of donkeys and colts, and an expense account supporting His ministry rather than carpentry work. This was bribery!

Just as we see in our day, times when bribery influence judges to make rulings, control politicians to pass unfair legislation, and coerce law enforcement to permit illegal activity, so was this black-market attempt by the tempter to manipulate Jesus! As a matter of fact, Jesus wouldn't have to worry about Calvary because Pilate would be in His pocket. He would have been able to tell Caiaphas what to do, because He would be the unofficial high priest. Jesus would own the entire religious and political system. This same attempt at bribery is being made to believers on a daily basis. How many times do we see Christians looking for public acceptance so much so that they refuse to stand against sin and are willing to compromise the gospel of Jesus Christ?

We cannot be so impressed with the world's system that we lose our identity in order to be a part of it.

The tempter has bribed the church with social acceptance, power, and influence. Today believers desperately want to be accepted, and they are willing to surrender (bow) to certain lifestyles in order to achieve this acceptance. Our worship must be to the Lord God! Our adoration must not be of political figures, celebrities, fortune companies, or media giants. We cannot be so impressed with the world's system that we lose our identities in order to be a part of it. This simply cannot continue. It is time for believers to stand up and let the clarion call of God be heard.

We will only bow to God and Him only will we serve. Any spirit that proposes modification of our Christian beliefs or that we bow out to public pressure and political correctness in order to gain access into certain circles is satanic. That is what Jesus judged the tempter to be. This tempter probably didn't look like Satan, but he sounded like Satan because of this proposal. That is why Jesus judged that spirit and called it Satan. This attempt at bribery wouldn't work on Jesus, and it should never work on us!

Chapter 7

CLOSING THE GATES!

Identity releases authority! Any authority given by God to man could only be released as God gave man His identity. Even in the book of Genesis, Moses records that God said, "Let us make man in our image, after our likeness: and let them have dominion over the fish of the sea and over the fowl of the air, and over the cattle, and over all the earth, and over every creeping thing that creeps upon the earth." Notice how God first gives man an identity that reflected His image and His likeness. *Then* God gave man authority and dominion. God never gave Adam and Eve authority until He first established their identity in Him. It is because identity releases authority. Notice that in Gen.1:27, the Bible declares "So God created man in his own image, in the image of God created he him . . ." Once again, the pattern is undeniable. The Bible doesn't just say that God created man and woman and then placed them over the garden.

The Bible is clear that male and female were

created in God's own image. Meaning, they were given an identity that could only be found in an eternally existent God. The next verse reveals the authority that God gave them afterward. "And God blessed them, and said unto them, be fruitful and multiply, and replenish the earth, and subdue it: and have dominion over the fish of the sea, and over the fowl of the air, and over every living thing that moves upon the earth." (Gen.1:28) Once again, identity releases authority!

An even greater example is found in the New Testament. Jesus asked the disciples in St. Matthew 16:13, "Whom do men say that I the Son of man am?" They began to say what others were saying about His identity. Then Jesus asked a very significant question, a question that promised to unlock destiny and release a new dimension of authority upon the earth. He asked them, "But who do you say that I am?"

Why was He so interested in what people were calling Him? Furthermore, why was He so interested in what the disciples were calling Him? It was because Jesus knew that the mission of His ministry was to build a powerful living organism called the church. All of His teachings, all of the miracles, and all of His sufferings centered upon establishing a universal body of believers who would spread His message and advance His Kingdom throughout the entire world. In order for the church to be successful, it must be empowered!

The Kingdom of God cannot be advanced through the hearts of people who are weaklings. It cannot be advanced through the lives of individuals who have no power. The message, the ministry, and the mission of Jesus Christ could only succeed when authority is released! Authority is released through identity, which is why Jesus asked those two questions. He wanted to empower these men with authority to advance His Kingdom and assist Him in building His church, but it rested upon them knowing who He was.

The first question would reveal what people were saying. The second question would reveal how much influence what people were saying had upon them. Notice what happened. Simon answered, "You are the Christ, the Son of the living God." The moment Simon released the revelation of Jesus' identity, Jesus released authority into Simon's life. First of all, Jesus answered him and said, "Blessed are you, Simon Barjona: for flesh and blood did not reveal it unto you, but my Father which is in heaven." (St. Matt.16:17) Jesus informed Simon that His identity wasn't made known through earthly means. This identity cannot be found through discovery, but rather through disclosure! Isn't that powerful? That is the reason why Jesus did not succumb to the tempter's incursion in the wilderness, when he tried to get Jesus to doubt His identity. It is because Jesus did not go through life trying to discover it. It was disclosed to Him by His Heavenly Father.

Whatever you discover, it requires logic. Whatever you receive through disclosure, it requires faith! God disclosed to Jesus who He was. That is why Jesus called Simon blessed. Simon was blessed because his faith received the revelation of Jesus' true identity. Secondly, Simon was blessed because he allowed the truth of what God disclosed to override the opinions of people who thought they knew Jesus' identity. Simon through revelation confirmed Jesus' Son-ship. Notice what knowing Jesus' identity did. Jesus tells Simon, "You are Peter, and upon this rock I will build my church . . ." What a powerful truth revealed in this text! The moment Simon called Jesus "Christ, the Son of the Living God" is when Jesus called Simon, Peter. All of this was locked within the truth of Christ's identity. Once this truth was revealed, it unlocked Simon's true destiny because identity releases authority!

Christ was revealing the mission for His ministry. He was on earth to restore mankind by building a body of believers who would express God in the earth. What Adam failed to do in the Garden of Eden, the Last Adam would successfully complete through His church. The first Adam was fruitful and multiplied, but he filled the earth with his Adamic nature.

As a result of this disobedient nature, sin entered and death was passed unto all men. However, the Last Adam would be fruitful and multiply, and His obedient nature would fill the earth, manifested through the church, and passing life to all who would receive Him. Jesus continues in telling Simon that He was going to build His church upon "this rock." The rock wasn't Peter. Simon was actually called "petros" in the Greek, which means a small stone. He tells Peter that upon this rock (Petra, which means a massive rock or a rocky cliff) He will build His church. Christ promised to build His church upon the revelation of His identity, assisted by the ones who would receive this revelation. Peter was now going to be an intricate part of this building because he represented all who would receive the revelation of Christ's identity.

Jesus is the chief corner stone—the stone which the builders disallowed (1 Peter 2:5). Peter's confession is the foundation to our faith, and Peter who confessed represents the small stones that would support this foundation. Jesus proceeds to tell Simon Peter that He would "give unto thee the keys to the kingdom of heaven: and whatever you bind on earth shall be bound in heaven: and whatever you loose on earth shall be loosed in heaven." This powerful verse reveals that Jesus gave His disciples authority!

They were now given permission by God to act on His behalf, and they could determine the activity on earth and in Heaven. That was the authority released to these men because they embraced the identity of Jesus. The moment Simon agreed with God concerning the identity of Jesus as the Christ and agreed with Christ concerning his own identity as Peter, he was given authority. Furthermore, Jesus called Simon a rock just like Himself, only a smaller version. Therefore, Simon Peter and the other disciples discovered that our identities are found only in Jesus.

How powerful is a body of believers when

it understands that its identity rests in Jesus! However, notice what Jesus reveals at the end of verse 18. Jesus declares that the gates of hell shall not prevail against the church. He acknowledges a warfare that is engaged between two kingdoms. He never said the gates of hell would not prosecute an attack. He just said the gates of hell would not prevail. This means that the church shall triumph. This means that the Body of Christ has already won, and this victory shall manifest in the end. This prophetic word from Jesus reveals the outcome of this warfare . . . we win! The gates of hell then aren't fighting to win, but rather fighting to incur as many casualties on their way to defeat. The devil already knows his future.

We must understand that if identity releases authority, then ignorance releases impotence!

Someone once said, "When the enemy reminds you of your past, remind him of his future!" Although this is a true statement, the problem really isn't the devil being reminded of his future. The problem is the church reminding herself of her identity in Christ. Too many professed believers are quitting and giving up in a war in which we are assured victory. It is because of a weak spirit that is being cultivated by a shrewd enemy. He is using our ignorance of our identity against us. We must understand that if identity releases authority, then ignorance releases impotence! If we are ignorant to our identity, then we will ignorantly assume another. This is where the enemy has been successful.

God on the Black Market

The gates of hell have unleashed an agenda in which believers can only identify with messages that speak to our sufferings, our pains, and our weaknesses. Believers want to commiserate, not come out of misery. This agenda only incubates an atmosphere and attitude of weakness, and it produces sympathy seekers not soldiers. No longer do believers relate to sermons pointing to their triumph in Christ, but only their tragedies and crisis.

The only way we can prevail against an encroaching enemy is to close the gates of hell that swing wide open with an agenda to rob us of our true identity. We must reject not only false doctrines and heresies, but also messages that incubate weakness and victimization. Only then will we be able to bind the spirit of guilt and shame and loose righteousness, peace, and joy in the Holy Spirit!

Marketing and Merchandising Misery

The gates of hell have marketed a product that is being sold not only through the secular media, but also through religious programming, books, and audio recordings. It is a mass marketing of misery. There are those who are merchandising misery in order to make a profit. It is a black-market scheme in which messages are presented to stir up emotions from past hurts and traumatic experiences in order to appeal to people's sense of hopelessness and desperation. It is because we are living in such perilous times in which tragedies are happening at a fevered pace. There are millions upon millions of people struggling with life situations, feeling hopeless in believing that things can get better.

That is why the message of the cross is a message of hope. That is why the gospel must be preached. It is because it provides healing for the wounds of the past. It places the guilt and the shame of past failures where they belong—in the past. It removes the feelings of hopelessness and despair, by giving people something to believe in. This isn't merchandising misery. This is offering a solution to the world's problems. I am thankful for ministries that reach out to the lost, the hurting, and those who have completely given up on life. I applaud the untiring efforts of spiritual leaders who are reaching millions with conferences and spiritual programming, as well as music and messages that heal and inspire. At the same time, I must recognize that everyone isn't in this Kingdom doing business for the King. There are those who seek to profit off other people's misery.

There are those who will manipulate messages to exploit the misfortunes of people, rather than presenting practical solutions from a biblical view. Many of these individuals profit by building dependency upon their ministry, rather than pointing the way to Jesus Christ. Please don't misunderstand me; there is nothing wrong with acknowledging our past hurts. There is nothing devious about exposing the abuses that have occurred in our lives, but this acknowledgment must accompany the realization that the will of Christ is for us to forgive, become strengthened, and move on into a life of helping others.

We cannot *remain* victims! The cycles of abuse and shame must end at some point once we receive Christ into our hearts. How many times must the same people attend the same conference, meeting, or seminar about the same issue? When will we accept by faith the healing that God has promised as our covenant right? How many years must we remain in the same place emotionally, psychologically, and spiritually, before we begin to walk into the life that Christ has made available? To many people, this may sound insensitive. To many people, these are not the words that should emanate from any ministry. That is why this marketing scheme is so successful, because it is just what people want to hear.

The nature of misery is that it loves both company and commiseration. It cannot be satisfied with being alone, neither is it satisfied with being temporary. It must attract attention and extend well beyond the borders of a healthy, human expression. It must go the extreme, in which the enemy uses it to cripple and grapple the individuals incubating it. This affects even the most sincere believer because it distorts his perception of his own identity. So the individual who has bought into this marketing scam can only identify with messages that relate to their suffering.

> **We cannot remain victims! The cycles of abuse and shame must end at some point, once we receive Christ into our hearts.**

They can't envision themselves beyond their pain, so any sermons that speak of our new life in Christ won't be received with faith. The truth is, we can only think of ourselves as long as we harbor misery. We can only agree with words that identify with our suffering as long as we commiserate. Words that speak of triumph aren't received like words that speak of tragedies. What is it about the human psyche that gravitates towards misery, even to the place where it accepts only negative reinforcements? What is it that keeps people revisiting the places of their hurts—that causes people to reenact their abuse—that prompts people to embrace songs and scenarios that are reminiscent of their pain? Why must we relive our sadness and reject the Word of God that teaches us how to triumph in Christ? When will we close the gates of hell that are spewing out venomous messages disguised as encouraging words, seeking to make us weaklings, not warriors?

Panhandling and Peddling Pain

It is hard to imagine that misery and pain would be the tools at the heart of the enemy's strategy. These are two experiences from which you would think people would naturally run. Unfortunately, it isn't the case. People are running toward these experiences because of what they bring. Misery and pain bring attention and sympathy! Unfortunately, we have grown up in an attention-deficit society, which has produced attention starvation, where people are doing some of the most extreme things in order to be recognized. The enemy uses the issues of our past to create an attitude of desperation and dependency in our present. Therefore, he streamlines his agenda through secular influences and carnal clergy in order to "peddle" pain, meaning the only messages we seem to hear involve things that we are "going through." These are sermons saturated with sufferings. Preachers are preaching to our pain, which is somehow bringing us pleasure. It is a deceptive tool of the enemy that will result in us covenanting with others solely based upon our wilderness experiences. This covenant will be a federation of weaklings perpetrating as spiritual believers, yet having no power to stand under pressure!

A powerful example of this is found in Joshua Chapter 9. There was a group of the inhabitants of Gibeon who heard about Joshua's conquest of Jericho and Ai. They were so afraid of being overtaken that they shrewdly devised a plan in which they pretended to be from a far country. They took old sacks and placed them upon their animals. They also took old wineskins that looked aged and worn, old shoes, torn garments, and bread that was dry and moldy, and with these they met up with the children of Israel.

The purpose of this scheme was to appear to be migrants who had wandered around destitute for a lengthy period of time in order to be granted protection by Joshua and Israel. The Bible states that the people of Israel did not seek counsel from God, but made a league with the Gibeonites. Israel was now bound by this agreement, later on discovering that these men were really their enemies disguised as impoverished ambassadors needing help. So now, they were obligated to allow these enemies to dwell among them, and they were morally bound to fight against anyone who rose up against the Gibeonites. This was an unholy alliance, but Israel was conned because the Gibeonites understood something that believers today are still ignorant of.

Issues attract issues! They dressed up as people who looked like they just came out of the wilderness, and Israel had just wandered forty years in the wilderness. The Gibeonites used a method that drew sympathy from Israel, because they could relate to pain and suffering. You see, as long as we allow the enemy to panhandle pain to us, our vision will be so skewed by our own sufferings that we will be unable to see even the most blatantly dishonest motives of other people. We become vulnerable targets as long as we commiserate and wallow in painful experiences. The only thing we will find ourselves doing is fighting wars that God didn't ordain for our lives. That is why these alliances only produce more pain and suffering. The only way to end this destructive cycle of pain is to overcome the sad memories of the things that caused it. This will settle the issues of our past and sever our alliances with people not ordained to go with us into our future.

> As long as we allow the enemy to panhandle pain to us, our vision will be so skewed by our own suf-

ferings that we will be unable to see even the most blatantly, dishonest motives of other people.

THE SPIRITUAL HUSTLE

The people of Israel considered themselves victims, and because they could not overcome the trauma of wandering in the wilderness forty years, they were hustled into an unholy alliance with ungodly Canaanities. This euphemism aptly describes the scam created and executed by the Gibeonites. It was a creatively devised plan to trap God's people into establishing a covenant agreement, thereby benefiting from the favor they had obtained with God. This hustle should have never worked, just as the spiritual hustle of the enemy should never work on us. We should never be misled into any unholy, unhealthy relationships, agreements, or partnerships. What makes us vulnerable is the feeling of victimization. The hustle is successful because God's people can only see the pains of their wilderness, not the glory of their survival. They can only lament over the abuses of their past, not rejoice over the fact that they are still alive. They can only commiserate in the failures of yesterday, not celebrate over the promises of tomorrow.

The reason this hustle should have never worked on the children of Israel is that they weren't the generation that died off. They should have left the wilderness grateful that God's intentions for them were good not evil and that a promised land awaited them. However, they inherited the feeling of victimization!

Just as millions of people all over the world are crying over past hurts and abuses, not realizing that they are the generation that God intends on delivering out of the cycles of abuse. People feel like victims based upon the violations and brutalities they suffered, not understanding that there are more victories awaiting them, than violations behind them. Another reason why this hustle of the Gibeonites should have never worked on the children of Israel is that they wandered for forty years and never saw moldy, dry bread. God fed them with fresh manna!

> **The hustle is successful because God's people can only see the pains of their wilderness, not the glory of their survival.**

They wandered in the wilderness for forty years and never saw old shoes covering their tired feet. Their shoes did not grow old or worn, neither did their feet swell. They wandered in the wilderness for forty years and never saw old wine bottles, old, rent, and bound up. God fed them with fresh water from a rock! The hustle was in getting them to feel so victimized that they sensationalized their wilderness wanderings.

They began to identify with pains they never suffered! They totally forgot about the merciful hand of God that sustained them even while in the wilderness. That is why the spirit of the victim must be bound in the lives of believers. It causes them to forget about the mercy of God and sensationalize the miseries of life. The moment an individual is hustled into receiving the mind of a victim, they begin to travel on a course of self-defeat, sensationalizing, and sorrow. We cannot allow the gates of hell to hustle us into believing that our situations are unique—that no one understands—that our pains are original, and that we can never overcome! We cannot begin to associate and covenant with others who choose to play the role of victim. The children of Israel should have recognized the "hustle game" of the Gibeonites and not allow them to trick them into making a league with them. However, discernment isn't possible as long as a victim's mentality is present. This was an Old Testament hustle that has been revised to ensnare the New Testament Church. More people are being spiritually hustled into fighting unnecessary wars, making unholy alliances, all because they refuse to be healed from the tragedies and traumas of the past.

Don't allow spiritual Canaanites to invade God's promises in your life. Don't let your hurts make you an eternal victim. Remember, it was the Lord that brought you out of your wilderness. Rejoice in the fact that you lived to see another day, and look forward to the glory of God being revealed through you as you conquer the giants of your past, present, and perhaps your future, and walk in victory!

Michael Lowery

The Children's Bread!

Emotional, psychological, spiritual, and physical healing all rest in the inheritance of the believer! It is possible to profess Christianity yet not possess this as a truth in your life. You will never take possession of anything, unless you first feel that you are entitled to it. All of us as ministers of the gospel preach about God's promises, yet few of us preach about entitlement. You see, entitlement is a major part of receiving God's promises for your life. Entitlement is the beginning of possession because it initiates the transaction! Messages about sufferings and trials must be accompanied with exhortations about the entitlement of every believer to live a life that is free from guilt and shame and to walk in the promises of God.

A victim doesn't feel they are entitled to better. It is one thing to acknowledge the pains of the past. It is another thing altogether to forfeit the rights of a better future. That is what makes the agenda of the gates of hell so extremely lethal. It robs the believer of their identity, causing him to disqualify himself from feeling entitled to the things of God. Nevertheless, Jesus reveals something that is powerful in St. Matthew 15: 26. This revelation is usually lost in the text because it is surrounded by other powerful verses. At this time, a Canaanite woman approaches Jesus because her daughter is "grievously vexed with a devil." This text then records the only time in which Jesus hears cries for help, yet doesn't say a word.

> **Entitlement is the beginning of possession because it initiates the transaction!**

His disciples even attempt to discourage her by begging Jesus to send her away. They were in essence telling her that she had no right to lay claims to any healing because she was not a Jew. This text continues describing this woman's persistence in that she cries out incessantly. Yet Jesus declares something so profound in verse 26 that it must not be overlooked.

Jesus tells the woman, "It is not good to take the children's bread and to cast it to dogs." Of course, we know how this story ends, with Jesus healing this woman's daughter at that very hour. However, it is what Jesus said in verse 26. He called healing "the children's bread." He also called doing what this woman requested of Him to do as "casting it to dogs." You see, before His death upon the cross, Divine Healing was excluded to God's covenant people, they being the Jews. As salvation was made available to everyone, whoever accepted Jesus as Lord and Savior and were baptized in Him, they became God's covenant people. Therefore, just as healing was a birthright to the children of Israel, now healing was a birthright to the children of God, or "spiritual" Israel.

The Body of Christ is now made a partaker of this Abrahamic Covenant, which promises healing and prosperity. That means that anyone who confesses Jesus as Lord is a seed of Abraham, an heir of God, and co-heirs with Jesus Christ. Healing becomes our covenant right. All healing can now be viewed as "the children's bread." It is what we can expect once we become a follower of Jesus. Therefore, to reject the promises of healing, to defer to our pain rather than God's power, is like letting the crumbs fall from our table.

The moment we open the gates of hell and subscribe to misery, pain, and victimization, we are letting the crumbs fall from our table. When the woman said that the dogs eat of the crumbs that fall from their master's table, she was acknowledging God's Divine Order in the Jews being first, for salvation came first to the Jews. She also acknowledged the Jews indifference to being first. She then acknowledged her willingness, as a Gentile, to become first in order to receive what they casually let fall from their grasp. Her faith revealed an invisible, allegorical picture of what was transpiring in the spiritual realm. This is what Jesus honored. Yet the truth is still the same! Healing is the children's bread. We must never forget that! To not acknowledge or receive our healing, but to choose rather to commiserate and accept messages about suffering and pain and to instead live like a victim is to let crumbs fall from the table. We must not allow the crumbs of His children's bread to fall into the cracks and crevices of life's most painful experiences!

THE WOUNDED HEALER

The Body of Christ seems to be at a loss on what to do with wounds and scars. We walk around feeling wounded and defeated, just because we suffered wounds and experienced defeat. In other words, we make syndromes out of setbacks and cycles out of circumstances.

We think that failures stigmatize our lives to the place where we can only identify with failures, but that just isn't true. Just because you have a scar, doesn't mean it has to hurt! Just because you have a wound, doesn't mean you have to walk around feeling wounded, nursing it and drawing negative attention to that area of your life or focusing on avoiding any and all contact.

We make syndromes out of set-backs and cycles out of circumstances.

I believe that every individual who seeks to be used of God must know how to effectively minister in the area of his or her own wounds. As a matter of fact, wounds and scars *must* become our aids in fulfilling God's purpose. The irony of this chapter is that the thing that is causing us to feel weak should be strengthening us. The thing that is causing us to disqualify ourselves should be qualifying and confirming our calling. Without misery, there can be no ministry! You must understand that adversity produces anointing. Wounds and scars are entryways through which the healing anointing flows! The greatest example of this is Jesus Christ. Consider the fact that His resurrection culminated over three decades of faithful service to His Heavenly Father. Also consider the fact that His resurrection permanently sealed His supremacy over death, hell, sin, and the grave, and it completed the sacrificial offering in which His blood was presented to God.

Finally, it established the superiority of Christianity to every other religious belief, with Jesus being the only central figure of any belief still being alive, after having once died. Yet the Bible declares that upon entering the room with His disciples, He showed Thomas and the others His wounds. He said, "Reach hither thy finger, and behold my hands; and reach hither thy hand, and thrust it into my side: and be not faithless, but believing." (St. John 20:27)

Why would Jesus do all of that during His resurrection, yet keep the wounds from His suffering? Surely, if He could get up from a grave with all power, then He could heal nail prints and a gaping spear wound. Undoubtedly, the same Heavenly Father who rolled back a great stone and raised Jesus from the dead could give Him a resurrected body that was free from injurious scars. To miss this revelation would be to miss one of the most important aspects of the resurrection. Jesus purposely kept His wounds!

His wounds were a testament of His sufferings and a confirmation that He was the same Jesus that once was dead. The same Jesus that died, rose again. Maybe that truth is so common in Christianity that it has lost its profundity. This wasn't another Jesus, nor was this a spiritual resurrection. This was a bodily resurrection of the same Jesus who was brutalized, humiliated, and crucified.

Yet here He was, standing in the middle of a room continuing His ministry on earth and preparing to ascend to a ministry in Heaven. Jesus, by keeping His wounds, confirmed that wounds and scars are profitable in convincing others that God raised you from the same grave of past hurts and humiliations. These are proofs that you've been wounded and scarred at some point in your life, but there is still purpose for you to fulfill. God wants to use *the same you* that was victimized and humiliated. He intends on healing you so completely that you become a healer for others. However, it is necessary that you still possess wounds as you heal others. They need to know that your past wasn't as glorious as your present. They need to see that you once lived what they perhaps are living now.

You see, oftentimes our anointing and our position are intimidating, and people don't know how to receive from us because they don't know how to receive us. To them, we appear to have it all together. God has to allow suffering in which there are permanent scars in order for us to relate to others. Our wounds are not defects or deformities, but they are Divine Reminders! They reveal to people as well as remind us where we've come from. Jesus was a wounded healer. For it was His stripes that healed us; it was His wounds that forgave our transgressions; it was His bruises that removed our iniquities.

The wounds were the portals through which

His healing anointing flowed. For all of us created in Him, we too must be wounded so that the healing power of God can flow through us and into someone else's life. Jesus tells Thomas to touch the areas of His wounding. He then tells Thomas to thrust his hand into His side. What a powerful word! It establishes a truth about our wounds: it is possible to have scars and still be healed. The pain didn't flow out of the touching or thrusting, but belief did!

God's people can talk about the events of their pasts. You can testify about the goodness of God even out of the situations that placed a scar on your life. There is truly nothing wrong with being scarred for life, because wisdom and belief, not pain, should come from it. Talking about your past and testifying about your traumatic experiences are like Jesus telling Thomas to thrust his hand into His side. The moment we embrace the revelation that we are wounded healers, we will close the gates of hell that distort all of the misery and pain of our past in order to prevail against our future!

Our wounds are not defects or deformities, but they are Divine Reminders!

Chapter 8

THE COUNTERFEIT CONSPIRACY!

The children of Israel learned a hard lesson revealed in our last chapter, when approached by the Gibeonites in Joshua, Chapter 9. They discovered that an enemy will pretend to be an ally or anyone else for that matter, in order to gain an advantage. We are never to underestimate the lengths our adversary will go to in order to plant a foothold in our life. The main point examined in this chapter is how authentic their façade appeared. They covered all the bases in appearing to be wandering ambassadors who came from afar. This ploy worked on Israel because of the issues they left unsettled. As a result, they entered into a covenant relationship with individuals God had not ordained for them. The covenant they had with the Gibeonites was based upon a lie! They fell for a counterfeit!

The success of any counterfeit operation is based upon how close it can come to looking like the real thing. This requires the counterfeiter to be able to copy the patterns, language, design, and overall personality of the original. This is a sophisticated operation that masterfully utilizes its familiarity with the identity of the original, integrating similar patterns and techniques, and developing an undetectable and untraceable plot to acquire the possessions of that unsuspecting victim.

Our adversary the devil has conspired to use relationships in order to fraudulently acquire the gifts, anointing, favor, and the blessings that God has released into our lives: for it is in relationships where he can get close enough to copy our patterns, language, overall personality, design.

We watched the devil attempt to coerce Jesus through temptations in the wilderness. Once again, every attempt in the wilderness failed, but this next level of warfare would be engaged through the relationships Jesus developed with His disciples. In relationships, where our defenses are ordinarily down, our discernment isn't usually heightened, and our most personal weaknesses are often exposed, is where we are the most vulnerable. When the devil gains an entrance into our lives, it commonly occurs through individuals with which we are connected.

The first time Jesus tells Satan to get behind Him occurred in the wilderness in St. Matthew 4: 10. The next time Jesus commands Satan to get behind Him occurred in St. Matthew 16: 23. This time, it didn't appear to be an obvious attempt by Satan, as before. This time revealed another level of warfare, in which the enemy used a trusted disciple who expressed great concern over Jesus' prophetic warning that He would be killed and raised again the third day.

> **When the devil gains an entrance into our lives, it commonly occurs through individuals with which we are connected.**

On the surface, Peter's response to Jesus' heart-wrenching words seemed genuine. Peter's words sounded like the words of a typical loved one when hearing such bad news; he sounded overwhelmingly concerned for Jesus' safety. Peter became alarmed and resolute in keeping Jesus from experiencing anything like what He had just foretold. To Peter, this just wasn't going to happen to Jesus. So when Peter rebukes Jesus in St. Matthew 16:22 and tells Him, "Be it far from thee, Lord: this shall not be unto thee," those words would ordinarily be considered words of endearment. However, Jesus didn't see them as that. As a matter of fact, Jesus saw it as the opposite. To Jesus, this was Satan influencing Peter! To Jesus, this was the counterfeit cries of a concerned friend and inwardly a carnivorous plot to stop the plan of God from being executed in the earth. Jesus discerned that Satan was using a trusted disciple to prevent Him from fulfilling His Father's will on earth.

Isn't it alarming how the enemy can perpetrate as a sincere supporter, yet is secretly seeking to rob God's people of their inheritance in Him? It is a counterfeit conspiracy to stop the plan of God that is so vast, by using the shallow means of relationships to undermine the steps God takes in achieving His ultimate goal.

The devil pretends to be an aide, a supporter, a trusted friend, a partner just to stop the will of the Father from being manifested. We must stop qualifying words based upon the relationship of the one speaking them. We must qualify the relationship of the one speaking based upon the words they use! As for Peter, I am sure he felt no evil intent when saying these words to Jesus.

It is quite possible that Peter was actually surprised by the stern words used by Jesus in response to his rebuke. His intentions were no doubt, honorable. Nevertheless, we must understand that even the best intentions become evil when they hinder the purpose and the progress of the will of the Father. Peter did not realize that his words stood adversarial to the cross, opposing the will of God that was to redeem lost Creation back to Him. Therefore, Jesus addressed the adversary who influenced these emotions.

Jesus acknowledged the same tempter who tried to influence Him in the wilderness. Satan was behind this outburst, and Jesus would once again command him back to where he belonged. If only believers would measure sincerity based upon how that particular gesture fits into the scope of God's plan, rather than how it makes them feel!

The moment we take our personal feelings out of the equation, we can successfully discern the motives behind the words. Jesus wasn't concerned about preserving a relationship with Peter or protecting Peter's feelings. As a matter of fact, Jesus wasn't even put off by the fact that Peter just earlier received a revelation from the Father concerning His Son-ship.

Jesus knew that just because a person can hear from God one minute doesn't mean they can't be influenced by Satan the next. The devil will use whomever he will to sow a seed of doubt when it comes to fulfilling God's assignment for us. We must judge the content of each and every conversation, not just those we are conversing with.

The devil can use a so-called "friend" to curse us, just as God can use an enemy to bless us. Once again, good intentions aren't enough. Peter's intentions seemed good, but Peter's intentions were evil, because they stood as an offence to Jesus. Obedience is the only thing that matters to God! Jesus dying upon the cross and being raised on the third day was His assignment that had to be completed no matter what!

You see, God is never influenced by our feelings or opinions when calling us to a specific work. Peter wanted to do something that even God didn't do. How dare Simon Peter cling to Jesus, when it was God who gave Jesus to the world? If God loved the world so much that instead of holding onto Jesus, He gave His only Son as a ransom for many, then Peter certainly had no right to hold Jesus hostage for the ransom of his own feelings! Believers everywhere must see a sophisticated, complex operation at work, in which the devil uses a method of counterfeiting in befriending us in order to undermine God's plan. Through these relationships, he will plant seeds to harvest the crop of forfeiture in order to abort God's purpose. Once we are able to discern this counterfeit conspiracy, we will begin to reevaluate the relationships we seek and redefine the ones we've already established.

OF GOD OR MEN

Jesus tells Satan to get behind Him. He was speaking to the spiritual influence that prompted Peter to rebuke Him. Jesus then declares something powerful at the end of St. Matthew 16:23. He said, "For you savourest not the things that be of God, but those that be of men." What exactly did Jesus mean? He was telling Peter that he did not have in mind the things that God desired, but the things that men desire.

He was telling Peter that he didn't perceive the things that God wanted, but that he was seeing things from an earthly perspective. Jesus did not only rebuke Satan, but He in essence explained the reason for the rebuke. Jesus was placing our feelings, emotions, and affections into two categories, either of God or of men. Either we are for Him, or we are against Him. The reason why this was Satan is because it was a minding of what matters to men. It was seeing from an earthly perspective, and not submitting to the will of the Father. This is manifested in positioning relational ties over the will of our Heavenly Father.

Relationships must be based solely upon the call of God for our lives! Unfortunately, saints do not covenant according to destiny. Saints covenant according to convenience, and all of the things that pertain to the senses. This is the opposite of why God ordained covenant relationship to begin with, starting with Adam and Eve in the Garden of Eden. Eve was created to be a helper to Adam. Meaning, God had purpose in mind when creating Eve for Adam. Their compatibility was based upon their God-given destiny.

Relationships must be based solely upon the call of God for our lives. Unfortunately, saints do not covenant according to destiny.

You see, we look for compatibility in every other area except God's divine purpose. It is only in the area of our calling that we make compromises. The things that are of men are centered upon feelings and emotions, with selfishness at its core. The things that are of men are bound by convenience and often desperation. They are limited to this earthly realm; therefore, they are things that are attractive to the senses. Jesus endeavored for His disciples to operate in another dimension, far beyond the senses. Jesus understood that this assignment in the earth required self-denial and humble submission to the complete will of the Father.

The relationships we have cannot place a

demand on us to defy God's will based upon any potential hurt and inconvenience this assignment would cause on the relationship. Feelings cannot be involved when it comes to obedience. The things that are of God abandon any and all sensual involvement, and they embrace the reality of the cost of our discipleship. Our adversary has conspired to make this assignment "mission impossible" by having us joined to individuals who often make it difficult, if not impossible, for us to fulfill the will of God.

No relational attachments should ever hinder the work of the Lord! To our society, this is fanaticism. They view Christianity through a perverted lens based upon extreme cases of tragedies dealing with the occult. Therefore, they scoff at any teaching that would express sincere and complete devotion to God, even above biological and social ties. They identify any religion as a cult if it isolates any person from their family or friends. Jesus never called for us to be isolated from anybody. It would be impossible to win them to Christ if we are. He does call for us to be committed to His Will, which often isolates us in their eyes. It is because of this commitment that the world hates Christianity. Yet this commitment is what Jesus requires in order for us to be His disciple.

Notice what St. Luke 14:26 declares. "If any man come to me, and hate not his father, and mother, and wife, and children, and brethren, and sisters, yea, and his own life also, he cannot be my disciple." When Jesus uses the word "hate," He is saying that we must love these relationships *less* than our relationship with Him. He is saying that we must love these individuals *less* than we love Him. This is a radical statement that isn't well received in many, many circles. Jesus understood that the enemy often uses relationships to hinder our progress as we seek to do the will of the Father, especially the relationships that are the closest to us, just like with Peter. We are vulnerable to Satan's influence if we don't put our loyalty to God's will even above our loyalty to any of these individuals.

Jesus even said in another passage of scripture, "My mother and my brethren are these which hear the word of God, and do it." (St. Luke 8:21) Notice how those words from Jesus reflected a mindset that liberated Him from any influence contradistinctive to God's plan for Him. No one could make Him forfeit this awesome and Divine Plan of God, regardless of how close he was to Jesus. Even as much as Jesus loved Lazarus, when He was called upon by Mary and Martha to heal Lazarus, who had become deathly ill, He stayed where He was until Lazarus had been dead four days. It is because Lazarus' destiny involved him being resurrected, not just healed. Therefore, Jesus wouldn't even let the love He had for Lazarus influence Him in interfering with Lazarus' destiny. Once we are resigned to place our Heavenly Father's will above all relationships, we establish a spiritual apparatus called discernment that determines the authenticity or counterfeisance of any and all relationships.

Michael Lowery

Covenant or Covet-knit

What binds us together? What are our relationships based on? When we strip our relationships down to their bareness, what lies at the heart of them? We will be shocked to learn that most relationships are established because there is something we are seeking from that individual.

Need is a motivating factor that often causes us to connect with others. At the center of this need is a covetousness that masquerades as friendship but seeks to absorb some part of another individual's life. This isn't necessarily about maliciousness, but rather about an unidentified need deep within our subconscious that desires something belonging to someone else. We all have been guilty of coveting at some point in our lives, some much more than others.

Sometimes it is easier to affiliate with someone who has what you want, rather than compete with them for it.

Our pride and pretense refuses to acknowledge this reality, but it is undeniable. This covetousness isn't based solely upon material things, for often people who have more materially are guilty of coveting the most. That is what makes coveting so deceptive. The moment this word is introduced, people generally point to desiring someone else's material possession. Yet coveting is dangerous because it isn't excluded to one particular thing.

A person may covet another person's boldness or intelligence. An individual may covet another person's independence or style. A person may even covet another person's anointing, faith, peace, or gifting. The list goes on and on. Without realizing it, we want these things so badly that we connect ourselves to those who possess them. Once again, it doesn't have to be with malicious intent. Of course, there is the obvious coveting that leads to murders, infidelity, theft, and so on. Coveting can be a monster on its own, without the jealousy and envy that it often produces, which takes an individual on an even darker course of discontentment and animosity. Sometimes it is easier to affiliate with someone who has what you want, rather than compete with them for it. Hence, relationships are often formed.

Ultimately, relationships end because that which has been coveted has been attained. Of course, the individual may say, "We no longer have anything in common." Even in dissolving marriages, people point to the fact that they just "grew apart." The reason for the high rate of divorce, the increasing number of broken fellowships, friendships, and partnerships, is because relationships were based upon covetousness; once an individual acquires what he or she covets, the relationship no longer has value. The truth of the matter is, we have a distorted view of covenant because we don't recognize that we are really coveting.

Coveting is based upon an attitude of "What can I receive?"

Covenanting is based upon an attitude of "What can I give?"

Michael Lowery

Not many people look at relationships from the perspective of how they can enrich that other individual's life. We look from a selfish perspective, at what we can get out of the relationship. However, the greatest example of covenant relationship is our Heavenly Father. He is a covenant-keeping God because He fully understands covenant. He knows that any covenant agreement is based upon an everlasting commitment to invest!

The reason God never breaks covenant is because He promises to always invest in the relationship; as long as He continues to invest Himself, the relationship will always live and flourish. That is why our earthly relationships die and dissolve; people stop giving of themselves. They think from the perspective of what they are not getting, rather than how much *they* are not giving. Peter's response to Jesus was based upon a covetous heart. He wanted Jesus to stay alive for his own personal reasons. This wasn't about the glorious resurrection that awaited Jesus. This wasn't about pleasing the Heavenly Father who sent Jesus. This wasn't about a lost world that needed Jesus. This was about Peter! Peter wanted for himself this Precious Gift that belonged to God, which God freely gave to the world! That is how shallow and narrow-minded the covetous heart is. It needs to be rebuked, because only Satan is behind it. That is why Jesus said, "Get thee behind me, Satan!" The truth is, Jesus did what Peter should have done.

The same way Peter received the revelation from God concerning Jesus' Son-ship is the same way Peter should have rejected emotions from the devil that opposed Jesus' mission. Peter had been given authority to bind and loose. He should have bound up that spiritual influence that used emotionalism as an attempt to derail the path that Jesus had to walk to get to the cross. What if Jesus embraced Peter's words and chose rather to appease a covetous spirit, instead of fulfilling the call of His Heavenly Father who sought to make covenant with mankind? What if Jesus felt so appreciative over the concerns of a friend that He forfeited His destiny on the cross? As absurd as that may sound, it is occurring daily.

People are surrendering the plan of God in order to make people happy. Believers are sacrificing the will of the Father in order to salvage a relationship. This is a counterfeit conspiracy that is sponsored by feelings that aren't based upon covenant, but covetousness. So because an individual is "knit" to another based upon what they are seeking, rather than "joined" based upon what God desires, they sacrifice God's will for their way. The moment we understand the purpose within every God-ordained relationship, we will commit ourselves to seeking the highest good of the individuals we are joined to and assist one another in fulfilling the will of the Heavenly Father.

Exposing an Imposter

There are many instances in the Bible where individuals disguised themselves so that they could gain an advantage. The Gibeonites used masterful trickery in order to enter into covenant with Israel. Jacob pretended to be Esau in order to obtain the blessing from Isaac. Tamar disguised herself as a harlot and slept with her father-in-law, Judah. Saul disguised himself to a woman at Endor in order to bring up Samuel from the dead.

The Bible is filled with instances of trickery that reveal how low an individual will go to achieve his or her selfish goals. If these lies can be devised by men, how much more will our adversary use lies in order to snare the believer?

In the New Testament age, the Body of Christ is dealing with "false apostles, deceitful workers, transforming themselves into the apostles of Christ." (2 Cor. 11:13) Paul even declares in verse 14 "And no marvel; for Satan himself is transformed into an angel of light." Paul tells the Corinthians that it is no surprise that men can perpetrate such fraud, because even the prince of darkness can pretend to be an angel from Heaven.

Paul reveals that even Satan has the ability to shed his "cloak of darkness" and put on the "garment of light." This revelation is so crucial to the Body of Christ because it informs us that we cannot presuppose how the enemy will come. We cannot assume what the devil will appear as. The reason Satan can "transform into an angel of light" is because he was at one time considered "son of the morning." (Isaiah 14:12) Satan can pretend to be an angel from Heaven because he fell from Heaven. If it is possible for Lucifer to become Satan, why isn't it possible for Satan to transform back into Lucifer? In other words, Satan may have lost his position in Heaven, but he hadn't lost his memory on how Heaven works. That is what makes him so dangerous. He can disguise himself as if God sent him. Therefore, we must "watch and pray."

What must we watch for? Paul reveals this in 2 Cor. 11:15. He says, "Therefore it is no great thing if his ministers also be transformed as the ministers of righteousness . . ."

Paul is saying it isn't difficult then since Satan can transform into an angel from Heaven; those he uses are able to imitate real ministers of Christ. This powerful verse reveals that they may preach truths of the gospel (love, forgiveness, peace, and positive things), yet Satan still influences them. They still find a way to deviate from the pure message of Christ, pointing back to themselves and worldly interpretations. [4] Paul concludes this verse by admonishing us to judge them according to their works.

We must not be deceived by miracles, charisma, intelligence, or oratorical skills. Paul declared that their "end shall be according to their works." Works will expose an imposter in ways that words cannot. That is what we are to watch for! The loyalty and commitment to Jesus Christ will be confirmed or denied by the works of these individuals claiming to be ministers of Christ. These works will eventually be self-seeking and self-gratifying, revealing the true nature of the spirit behind them. Remember, it was Lucifer who became self-seeking, as he sought to ascend above the heights of the clouds and desired to be like the most High.

> **Not only can individuals become imposters posing as ministers of Christ, thoughts can be imposters posing as missions for Christ!**

This same motive is reproduced in those Paul described as "Satan's ministers," because they will continue in this depraved pattern of fulfilling selfish ambitions and selfish desires. Not only can individuals become imposters posing as ministers of Christ, thoughts can be imposters posing as missions for Christ! We must also watch that we aren't influenced by thoughts or reasoning that exalts itself against the knowledge of God.

The obedience of Christ exposes every pretentious thought or opinion regarding our decisions. Therefore, when we walk in complete obedience, we expose every adversarial plot of the enemy by revealing the true identity and source of his hindering agent, whether it is a man or a mindset!

Profit Gains and Losses

The spiritual ledger of the enemy measures profit gains and losses under a much different margin than we at first believed. The spreadsheet of his black-market accounts has revealed another area in which his kingdom's net worth has steadily increased. Of course, we know that the adversary desires souls. He wants to take as many people with him into eternal damnation as possible. However, with all of our focus being entirely upon soul winning, we have completely ignored a very important aspect of his kingdom's success. When an individual dies, the main concern usually voiced by the eulogist at the funeral is whether that individual made a commitment to the Lord Jesus Christ before death. The focus is always on the soul "being right with the Lord!" Not much is asked about whether an individual fulfilled God's destiny for his life. No one ever mentions if that deceased person walked in his God-given purpose.

For some reason, the Body of Christ has considered Heaven the final reward. Eternity with Christ is our final destination; rewards for our works are the final reward! This is the area where the adversary knows our ignorance abounds. He continues to prosecute an all-out assault against the Body of Christ to prevent believers from walking in purpose and fulfilling destiny. The kingdom of Satan measures profit gains and losses based upon the number of people who die outside of Christ *and* the number of people who are in Christ, yet die outside of destiny.

This margin represents his profit-gains margin. The profit-loss margin to the devil is the people who receive Christ *and* the believers who walk in purpose and fulfill destiny. Therefore, we *must* stop looking at salvation as the end of our journey, culminating with Heaven. We must see salvation as the beginning of our journey, leading us into a life of purpose and destiny, culminating with eternity with Christ!

The greatest tragedy in life isn't based upon the type of suffering that precedes death; the greatest tragedy in life is death preceding destiny. Believers seem to be ignorant to this truth. We forge relationships that hinder our walk; we embrace ideologies and philosophies that influence our minds against the knowledge of God, and we allow our past to keep us from walking into our future. There are so many instances in scripture that express this truth. Two of the greatest examples are Jonathan and of course, Samson. Jonathan is best known for his covenant with David.

The Bible declares that the love that Jonathan had for David surpassed that of the love of women. When David hears of the news of Saul and Jonathan's death, he laments with great mourning. The book of 2 Samuel Chapter 1 describes this very intimate time of grieving in David's life. He declares something powerful in verse 25–27. David says, "How are the mighty fallen in the midst of the battle! O Jonathan, you were slain in your high places. I am distressed for thee, my brother Jonathan: very pleasant were you unto me: thy love to me was wonderful, passing the love of women. How are the mighty fallen, and the weapons of war perished." David grieves over Jonathan, calling him mighty. He also declares that the weapons of war perished. He understood that Jonathan had no business being slaughtered like an animal in Mt. Gilboa and then hung on a wall as a trophy of the Philistines. This was a tragedy. This wasn't just a horrible death to a friend, but this was a perishing or wasting of the weapons of war.

Jonathan should have been with David, the anointed king of Israel. Jonathan was in covenant with David, but notice with whom he died. Jonathan was killed with his father and his brothers. God had removed the throne from Saul, yet Jonathan couldn't remove himself from Saul's life. Because earthly relational ties were stronger than the purpose and destiny God had for Jonathan, he wound up dying a horrible, gruesome death. Jonathan had moments in which we saw glimpses of great potential, yet they pale in comparison to what might have been.

It is unimaginable what great exploits were awaiting Jonathan and David had they both been a tandem during David's reign. Jonathan no doubt would have led David's mighty men of valor, but here was Jonathan hanging upon a wall in Bethshan, along with his father. Here was Jonathan a world apart from his God-given destiny, all because he wouldn't disconnect himself from his rebellious father.

The enemy measures profit gains and losses, based upon destiny gained or lost.

The truth of the matter was, Jonathan should have been the next king, but even Jonathan accepted the fact that the anointing was upon David, and he was willing to serve him. Therefore, Jonathan possessed great character as well as a warrior spirit. The mighty had fallen, and weapons of war had perished!

It was a waste of purpose and potential! This is how the enemy measures profit gains and losses, based upon destiny gained or lost. If only we understood that relationships could help or hinder our walk into the path that God has predestined for us.

How many weapons of warfare are perishing because they remain unused due to tragic forfeiture of purpose and destiny? How many graveyards are filled with untapped potential and unreached destinies? We must recognize this black-market attempt of the enemy to get us to embrace God, but reject His sovereign plan for our existence. In this way, our adversary is willing to take a loss in the area of a soul not entering into eternal damnation, but take a gain in a soul never reaching his Divine Destiny.

The Delilah Device

Samson is another great example of destiny being lost. Most people point to the one passage of scripture in Judges 16:30 where the Bible records "And Samson said, let me die with the Philistines. And he bowed himself with all his might; and the house fell upon the lords, and upon all the people that were therein. So the dead which he slew at his death were more than they which he slew in his life." We read this one verse, and we view it as the fulfillment of the prophetic word that God sent to Samson's parents that he would begin to deliver Israel out of the hand of the Philistines. This verse in Judges 16 cannot be viewed in the positive light of prophetic manifestation, but in the dark shadows of a tragic end to great promise and potential. Samson should not have been in Gaza, eyes gauged out, bound with fetters of brass, and grinding in a prison house.

> **We should not want our lives to be reduced to a flash flood of a few, fine finishes or a preliminary preview of potential and promise.**

Samson should not have been asking God to strengthen him one more time so that he could avenge the Philistines for what they did to his two eyes. Samson should not have been reduced to standing as a spectacle for the Philistines' entertainment. Samson's potential and purpose were too great to end up begging a lad to hold his hand so that he could lean upon two pillars. This wasn't a fulfillment of a prophetic word; this was a glimpse of a greatness that never was! Before we go looking at an individual's accomplishments and deeming them as successful, we must consider how God views success—not based upon what we have accomplished, but what He has predestined us to accomplish! We should not want our lives to be reduced to a flash flood of a few, fine finishes or a preliminary preview of potential and promise. Samson's life ended in a tragedy, which typifies how the black market of Satan works.

It wasn't enough for Samson to be born with great destiny. He needed to have possessed enough character to control his passions, which would have given him the power over his proclivities. Even in that, Samson was able to use his strength to overcome those who tried to kill him. He was a functioning addict, with lust being his addiction, and could use his strength to get out of the most harrowing situations. With his strength, at one point he slew thirty men in Ashkelon; he later killed a thousand men with a new jawbone of an ass.

All of these exploits displayed the great strength and potential of Samson who judged Israel twenty years. Because of his proclivity for women, this weakness found him in a cycle of needing to use his physical strength in order to escape life-threatening situations. Although he was strong physically, he was weak morally. Samson thought that he could continue this pattern of reckless behavior and could easily summon his strength to rescue him.

Samson did like many of us who feel because we have a connection to God that our position gives us a license for loose behavior. At any moment like times past, we can easily summons the Holy Spirit, who will give us the strength we need to get out of foolish and reckless situations. However, Samson learned a tragic lesson, recorded in Judges Chapter 16. Samson learned there was a device of Satan who was named Delilah.

The Delilah device isn't just about a woman that Samson's destiny tragically collided into. The Bible records in 2 Corinthians 2:11 "Lest Satan should get an advantage of us: for we are not ignorant of his devices." This verse tells us that there are specific schemes and strategies that the devil uses of which we must be aware. These schemes are both dangerous and masterful because they transcend generational, racial, and cultural boundaries. These devices have worked successfully throughout the course of history and must be exposed so as not to ensnare the believer.

The Delilah device is one of those schemes and can be revealed in Judges 16:4. The Bible declares "And it came to pass afterward, that he loved a woman in the valley of Sorek, whose name was Delilah." The Delilah device involves an emotional attachment, which makes a believer vulnerable. You see, this was the first time that Samson's heart was involved. When an individual's heart becomes involved, they are even more susceptible to Satan's influence.

This temptation is unlike any other, because it isn't just about satisfying an urge or impulse. This temptation is tied to an emotional attachment! Even though choosing Delilah was in direct disobedience to the command of God, this was what Samson wanted. His love for Delilah not only caused him to justify his actions, but ignore the signs that she was a counterfeit.

That is how lethal the Delilah device is; it perpetrates as something real so that it can obscure any realizations or revelations of it being a counterfeit! This was about much more than being what Samson wanted. This was about being what Samson felt he *needed!* That is what makes the Delilah device such a choice device of Satan.

Michael Lowery

The Delilah device perpetrates as something real so that it can obscure any realizations or revelations of it being a counterfeit!

Delilah represents a spiritual influence that has the power to influence other individuals in order to manipulate and control a believer. A believer then gives this individual complete access to their most intimate feelings, private thoughts, and personal desires. Delilah, in the spiritual realm, is a specific device or strategy that influences a person, not the actual person. Delilah isn't about a woman or even a man for that matter. Think about it! Samson loved Delilah, but the Bible never says she loved him. As a matter of fact, she conspired with the Philistines for eleven hundred pieces of silver *apiece* in order to reveal the source of his strength. Delilah stood to become a very rich woman, and all she had to do was entice Samson.

She was involved in a counterfeit conspiracy to ensnare Samson, which was how he ended up in Gaza, bound with fetters of brass, grinding in the prison, with his eyes gauged. Yet even before this, Samson had every opportunity to leave Delilah.

Three times he told her where his strength supposedly was, and on three occasions she had people waiting to bind him when they thought this information was correct. Because of Delilah's influence, he could not break free! His heart was involved. Eventually, he revealed the true source of his strength, and she was able to have this incredibly strong man subdued and captured. At this point, he could no longer summon his strength like in times past because his hair had been cut; meaning, he was disconnected from the source of his strength!

The enemy will use a spiritual Delilah as a device to ensnare God's people, for this device will disconnect us from God's presence, which is where the fullness of joy is received and where we get our strength! We must walk in obedience that keeps us connected to our Heavenly Father and not become vulnerable to this wicked strategy—lest we allow the devil to take advantage of us and we find ourselves like Samson performing a closing act to a tragedy instead of the opening act to God's destiny!

Chapter 9

THE SPREADING DEMOCRACY

Our world is like an ever-changing landscape. Nations that have long held ironclad systems of governments are abandoning their philosophies and embracing the tenets of democracy. More nations are ending their histories of monarchy and dictatorship and are adopting democratic governments. As this book is being written, a war is being waged in Iraq by a coalition led by the United States to rid the world of a cruel regime ruled by Sadam Hussein and to establish a democratic government for the Iraqi people. While there are those in Middle Eastern and Far Eastern countries that oppose democratic governments, there has never before in the history of our world been such a major influence of one type of government as the spreading of democracy. The United States and many of its allies are touting democracy as the universal choice of government: a government of the people, for the people, and by the people. The U.S. and millions of others around the world believe that wherever people posses the right to vote they are insured the protection of civil liberties and freedoms.

This twenty-first century is seeing a widespread of democracy all across the world. Of course, as a citizen of the United States of America, I appreciate the freedoms that make this country a great nation, freedoms that my family and I now enjoy. As a concerned citizen, I always exercise my right to vote in order to invest in the future of America. Therefore, I stand as a proponent of democracy, fully aware of many of its imperfections and flaws, completely confident that this system of government arguably surpasses any and all other existing governments around the world.

However, as a citizen of the Kingdom of God, I am terribly concerned about the democratic influence upon the Body of Christ. Democracy is spreading fast, even within the Body of Christ, at epidemic proportions. The problem with a democracy is that it is adversarial to the advancement of God's Kingdom. Democracy may be good for our society, but it is detrimental to the Kingdom of God! God's Kingdom has a system of government that isn't based upon a democracy, but a theocracy. God's Kingdom isn't people ruled; it is a Kingdom that is God-ruled! Believers today are casting their votes to determine the next move of God. People are using the ballot boxes of their logic in order to make important decisions regarding their futures.

> **The problem with democracy is that it is adversarial to the advancement of God's Kingdom.**

The reason many trials and tribulations befall believers is that they refuse to acknowledge God in all of their ways and allow Him to direct their paths. Because they are determined to "legislate" their own lives with reasoning and arguments, they find that their wisdom still isn't good enough to navigate their ways through life. The problem is that very few people understand how important government is to Christ.

Jesus came to establish His government in the earth, which was nothing at all like the government that the Jews were expecting the Messiah to establish. They were expecting the Messiah to overthrow the current Roman government, yet Jesus' ministry centered upon an invisible sphere of God's influence. The Bible declares in Isaiah 9: 6 and 7 "For unto us a child is born, unto us a son is given; and the government shall be upon His shoulder: and his name shall be called Wonderful, Counselor, the mighty God, the everlasting Father, the Prince of Peace; of the increase of His government and peace there shall be no end, upon the throne of David, and upon His kingdom, to order it, and to establish it with judgment and with justice from henceforth even for ever. The zeal of the Lord of hosts will perform this."

What a powerful passage of scripture! Isaiah prophesied that the power and authority (government) would rest upon Him. The prophet Isaiah also revealed that this authority and power, along with His peace, should increase and never end. What Jesus carried along with Him was a burden for His Father's will and a heavy zeal to establish God's government in the earth. This would happen in lieu of governments already being in place. Jesus' goal wasn't to overthrow existing governments; He did not come to unseat current authority, neither did He come to coexist and cooperate *with* the current political system.

Jesus came to establish and increase His government *within* governments. His government is invisible and intangible, empowering its citizens who, through faith, submit to its laws. Yet the citizens of the Kingdom of God are subject to the laws of the land. That is why meekness is what characterizes the citizens of God's Kingdom—meekness not weakness!

We possess the power and authority of God, yet it is under the control of the Holy Spirit! The reason is so that no citizen of God's Kingdom can disregard the laws of the land and disrespect the authorities that govern these laws, as long as these laws do not defy the laws of God. Yet God's Kingdom has its own agenda. God's Kingdom has its own laws, language, economy, and citizenship.

That is why these governments often collide! Because of the fact that Jesus' government is established within current governments, there are often conflicts in the philosophical differences of these governments.

Those who are citizens of a democracy will find themselves influenced by the democratic philosophy and unable to submit to an invisible, theocratic government. That is why we cannot be conformed to this world. We cannot allow the world's philosophies and ideologies to influence our way of thinking pertaining to the Kingdom of God. As long as we refuse to renew our minds to a theocratic government in which God's sovereignty rules our lives, we will continue to protest the fact that we must allow Him to govern us, even without our vote!

SPIRITUAL SUFFRAGE

The greatest aspect of the democratic government is voting. This is the impetus that empowers democracy, because it gives every citizen the power to determine who serves in political office to represent and advance his own personal and political interests. Every race, culture, business, and class of people possess their own interests. No one ever votes according to someone else's interest! Individuals always cast their vote for candidates that make campaign promises based upon issues that relate to them, not somebody else. It wouldn't make sense to elect a candidate whose views you oppose. It is impractical to support an individual whose platform contradicts the values you embrace. Therefore, voting is done through the shallow, narrow lens of one's own interest. Although there is no "I" in the word "vote," selfishness is the "eye" of voting! Because voting is the cornerstone to the democratic government, wherever democracy reigns, the attitude of selfishness rules! That is why democracy is adversarial to the government of Christ.

People oppose the plans of God when those plans oppose their own interests. Because God doesn't wait for our votes to decide His will for our lives, we refuse to submit to His will when it conflicts with what we desire. We cannot relate to a government that decides our future!

Our democratic influence continues to fight against the will of our Heavenly Father, because somehow we feel we must have a voice in the direction our lives are to go. God's job isn't to serve our interests! Since we didn't vote God into the office of Creator, we cannot vote Him out! God doesn't need our votes to determine His will for our lives, but we need to agree with His will for our lives in order for His will to be fulfilled.

Just because God's plans don't serve our interests doesn't mean that God's plans aren't in our best interests.

Our voting privileges end in the spiritual realm. In the spiritual realm, voting only leads to a way that seems right to a man, but the end is the way of death (Prov.14:12). Spiritual suffrage leads to spiritual suffering! Spiritual voting is placing one's opinion along with the opinions of others above the will of our Heavenly Father. Just because God's plans don't serve our interests doesn't mean that God's plans aren't in our best interests. What makes God's government so profound is that it is a theocracy without being a dictatorship. God rules our lives . . . with our cooperation! Therefore, as we submit to His will and His ways, we invite His government to rule us and His blessings to overtake us!

THE POPULAR VOTE

Our lives are governed by popular opinion. We measure what is right based upon the majority. The popular vote is a black-market attempt to get us to believe that God is moving us in a certain direction, using people's opinions as confirmation! With the consensus, we tally up what is a considered the will of God, and we accept it as being what God wants because it is what the majority believes. What we don't realize is that God's voice isn't the minor voice of the majority, but a major voice in a minority! When we look to the popular vote to elect what God has destined as His will for us, then we will miss God!

The children of Israel reveal to us this tragic example of going by popular opinion in determining one's own future. In the book of Numbers, Chapter 13, the Bible records that Moses sent twelve spies to Canaan to see the land that God had promised to give to them. The twelve spies went up, searched the land, and came back with one cluster of grapes so big they had to carry it with people holding it upon a staff. They also brought back pomegranates and figs. Nevertheless, an interesting thing happened when returning to give the report concerning the land. Ten of the spies gave an unfavorable report, while two of them (Joshua and Caleb) confirmed that they were well able to take the land.

> God's voice isn't the minor voice of the majority, but a major voice in a minority!

The ten spies confirmed the fact that the land flowed with milk and honey, and they showed the people the fruit. Yet they stressed that the people in the land were strong, and that the cities were walled and very great. They told the multitudes that they saw the sons of Anak, which were considered giants, and that they were grasshoppers in their own sight, as well as in the sight of the giants. This stirred up the congregation so much so that they murmured against Moses, wanting to kill him. This passage of scripture reveals the beginning of a democracy.

The people decided that they weren't able to go up, even after God told them the land was theirs. They believed the popular opinion of the ten, rather than the two who believed they were well able to take the land. Unfortunately for Israel, the popular vote won the election of forfeiture! This resulted in a 40-year term in the wilderness. The moment this vote was cast by the majority, it won in the minds of the congregation. Perhaps if only the two said they were as grasshoppers, and the ten said they were well able, the favorable report would have been believed. I truly believe the negative report won out because the majority rules. I am sure the people considered the words of Joshua and Caleb as just opinion, but the words of the ten as fact; all because these words were the consensus of the majority, while the report of the Lord rested in the voices of the minority.

Do you see how this popular vote mentality can abort God's plan? That is why God chooses for us, rather than letting us take a public opinion poll to decide His plans for our lives. Otherwise, we will be like the children of Israel, voting ourselves out of the place of promise!

The Electoral College

The spies were sent under one government, and came back campaigning for another. According to the book of Numbers, Chapter 13, God, through Moses, sent the twelve spies out to search the land of Canaan. Meaning, this assignment was given under a theocratic government. God was governing the children of Israel. God was deciding their fate. God was ordering their steps, and He had chosen this method to confirm for them that this land was indeed the land that He had chosen. Yet as ten of the twelve spies went out, in forty days they moved from a theocratic government to a democratic government. The spies were now part of an electoral college that was appointed to represent the voice and popular vote of the majority of the people of Israel. Thus by the time they returned and gave the report, it was a representation of how the majority of them felt about themselves. You see, the problem with the ten was that fear, not war, was in their hearts. The problem with the ten was that they had an inferiority complex. The ten spies already saw themselves as grasshoppers, so when they saw the giants, it just gave them an excusable opportunity to project this perception, and it reflected the opinions of the entire congregation.

The multitude of the children of Israel already had issues with their identities due to the years of captivity. Therefore, the ten spies cast a vote that represented the popular vote of the congregation, choosing to elect the negative report over the positive. The negative report was an extension of a negative perception the entire congregation already possessed! That is why we must reject the voices of popular opinion. The individuals spewing these negative words are just representing negativity that occurred in their past, things they hadn't settled. These are the individuals that Satan has "elected" to enlist feelings of fear and reservation. The enemy wants us to register our own hurts and feelings, nominate our opinions by exalting them against the knowledge of God, and then voting along with these individuals for our own opinions to rule us rather than God's will. Joshua and Caleb knew that the ten weren't speaking the mind of God. That is why they voiced their defiance against this popular opinion. More believers ought to be like Joshua and Caleb and not allow the opinions of people to rob them of their inheritance, but stand upon what God has purposed and see things from His perspective.

> So the ten spies cast a vote that represented the popular vote of the congregation, choosing to elect the negative report over the positive.

"Bye"-Partisanship

Democracy just doesn't work in the Kingdom of God! Though it may be highly regarded in Western civilization and spreading in its influence across the world, it brings woeful results to the life of a believer. We are simply unable to vote outside of our own interests! We must abandon the philosophical influence of democracy that places the power and authority into the hands of people. People, when left to their own devices, will self-destruct. We must answer to an authority that is greater than ourselves, who sees far beyond our limited view and sphere of influence, and who holds us accountable to a higher standard, both morally and ethically. The truth of the matter is the greatest flaw in a democratic government is partisanship.

Democracy polarizes a society to the place where it classifies people according to their interests. This polarization is called partisanship. Political parties have long been a staple of democracy and have led to filibustering, governmental gridlocks, and negative campaigning, just to name a few. Democrats fight to defend the Democratic interest, while Republicans war to defend the Republican interest.

The independents and other burgeoning parties are shouting loud to simply be heard.

While people are voting party lines, accepting only candidates that represent their political party, America is nationally divided. This partisanship has placed a stranglehold on democracy in such a way that it has become a political circus!

Partisanship is nothing more than political partiality. I have never heard, in any civilized conversation, a person taking a side on an argument . . . way before the conversation actually begins! That example represents the foolishness of partiality. It means that someone has already chosen a point of view; they have already taken a strong position before any subject is ever presented. Do you understand how insidious that is? When an individual does this, they completely rob themselves of the ability to see the whole picture. His vision will always be narrowed to his own vantage point. Who only wants to see in part? Who only wants to understand in part? Who in his right mind only wants to surround himself with people who only see from the perspective of his own self-interests? That is the democratic flaw that weakens this powerful country in ways that transcend our financial and military strength. When this principle is transferred into the spiritual realm, you can see how this can translate into spiritual weakness. Spiritual partisanship results in an individual only seeing in part.

Spiritual partisanship is in an individual using earthly wisdom to review the facts of one's self-interests, rather than using God's wisdom to reveal the truth of His will. They will always remain partial to their point of view, surrounding themselves with people who share and support their point of view. That means they could be walking in the spirit of error, but estranged from any voice that could speak truth into their lives. This is what I coin "Spiritual partisanship!" It is steeped in earthly wisdom that opposes the wisdom of God, especially since God's wisdom is without partiality (James 3:17) and often conflicts with their limited perspective. They have taken a position before they understand fully the will of the Heavenly Father! They have postured themselves to only hear words that coincide with their views, rather than opening their spirit-man to receive the truth of God's Word.

When a person has an opinion and stands upon that opinion, regardless of how it conflicts with the Word of God and in spite of how it negatively affects the working of God's greater plan, he is spiritually partisan. He has voted his way as the way he will follow and has muted the voice of godly wisdom. This is what happened in Saul's life in the Old Testament. He was partial to his own way, even after being told by Samuel to completely destroy the Amalekites and leave nothing behind. Saul opted to invade these people, keep the things he considered valuable and important, and then destroy the things he felt were no good.

He kept the best and destroyed the worst. Yet Samuel came to Saul and told him that this was rebellion because he didn't do as God commanded. Saul's actions were the result of an attitude that reflected a partiality to one's own will. He even took the things he saved from this invasion and offered them to God for a sacrifice. Samuel asked Saul if God had more pleasure from sacrifices than obedience. Samuel revealed to Saul that obedience is better than sacrifice and to listen was better than the fat of rams. In other words, God wants us to obey Him, rather than try to appease Him with things that come from our own way.

When a person has an opinion and stands upon that opinion, regardless of how it conflicts with the Word of God and in spite of how it negatively affects the working of God's greater plan, he is spiritually partisan.

God isn't impressed with offerings that derive from a life of disobedience and rebellion, regardless of how much they seem to be worth. *The best of the worst is still nothing more than the worst at its best!* That is why we must abandon any view that opposes the plan of God. We must reject this black-market attempt of the enemy that attempts to bribe God with an offering that substitutes obedience.

We must forsake this spiritual democracy that influences a partisan attitude, rather than encourages an available spirit. The moment we submit to the Lordship of Jesus Christ and allow Him to govern us, our actions will shout "good-bye!" to partisanship, and welcome a much-needed, always-stable, theocratic government. This God-rule will never leave us in the deficit of defeat, but will lift us to a surplus of successful living by balancing the budget of our inadequacies, with the abundance of His sufficiency!

Bibliography

ID Theft: What's It All About The Federal Trade Commission (FTC)-www.consumer.gov/idtheft.com or write: Identity Theft Clearinghouse, Federal Trade Commission, 600 Pennsylvania Avenue, NW, Washington, DC 20580

ID Theft: When Bad Things Happen to Your Good Name The Federal Trade Commission November 2003 www.ftc.gov or write: Federal Trade Commission, 600 Pennsylvania Avenue, NW, Washington DC 20580)

Contact Information

Pastor Michael A. Lowery
c/o Berean Christian Fellowship
3925 North Martin Luther King Blvd. Ste. #211
North Las Vegas, NV 89032
E-mail address: lowerypm@aol.com
Or berean@lvcm.com

Endnotes

ID Theft: What's It All About The Federal Trade Commission www.consumer.gov/idtheft.com

ID Theft: When Bad Things Happen To Your Good Name The Federal Trade Commission November 2003 www.ftc.com

ID Theft: When Bad Things Happen To Your Good Name The Federal Trade Commission Identity Theft Clearinghouse Federal Trade Commission, 600 Pennsylvania Avenue, NW, Washington, DC 20580

ID Theft: What's It All About? Federal Trade Commission www.consumer.gov/idtheft.com

Full Life Study Bible

Order more copies of this book at

TATE PUBLISHING, LLC

127 East Trade Center Terrace
Mustang, OK 73064

(888) 361 - 9473

Tate Publishing, LLC

www.tatepublishing.com